Overcoming Common Problems Series

Overcoming Common Problems Series

Overcoming Common Problems

Depression at Work

Vicky Maud

Published in Great Britain in 2000 by
Sheldon Press
Holy Trinity Church
Marylebone Road
London NW1 4DU

British Library Cataloguing-in-Publication Data

A catalogue record for this book is available from the British Library

ISBN 0–85969–830–0

Typeset by Deltatype Limited, Birkenhead, Merseyside
Printed in Great Britain by
Biddles Ltd, Guildford and King's Lynn

Contents

This book is dedicated with love to my dear daughter-in-law, Toni.

Acknowledgements

As an agony aunt it never ceases to surprise me how supportive and generous my readers and listeners are when it comes to providing me with case histories and information for my books. This time was no exception. I was inundated with letters and my first thanks must go to each and every one who wrote in. They know what it is like to suffer with depression in the workplace and by sharing their experiences hope to ease the suffering of others.

Over the past few years I have worked very closely with Depression Alliance, the National Depression Campaign and the Royal College of Psychiatrists, and without their help, information and support this book would not have been completed.

Acknowledgements also to Masters and Johnson for information.

My warmest thanks go to Margaret who typed my manuscript superbly while listening to my often flagging voice on tape, and to my friends Ann and Wendy who were always at the end of the phone when I neded someone to tell me that I didn't need that extra hour in bed and should be up working on my book instead!

Last but by no means least, thanks to my husband, Ken, and children, Philip, Louise, John and Lucy, for their constant love and encouragement.

Foreword

Dear Friend,

Someone once said to me that you have to experience depression to really understand the hell it can put you through and I know that is true. Although my personal bouts of depression were shorter than many people suffer I shall never forget the nightmare feelings I had at the time.

It was a bit like travelling through a dark tunnel, alone, scared and not wanting to go forward but unable to turn back. Each evening I just wanted the dark to swallow me up into a deep sleep, desperately hoping that things would be different the next day, but they never were. Both my bouts of depression were work-induced, doing jobs I hated and being pushed around by people who felt this was their mission in life. It gave them a sense of importance with no thought for those whose lives they made a misery.

Before I had a family I worked for an American bank in London where the stress levels in the foreign exchange department soared, leaving me and others feeling like wrung-out dishcloths by the end of the day. The department was run like an army mission – we were the soldiers and the officers were there to be obeyed. The manager I worked for did not help by trotting out his daily quote as we left the office each evening. 'Another day gone, another day nearer the end,' he would say mournfully. I was hardly out of my teens and this certainly was not what I wanted to hear. Yet all these years later I have never forgotten them or the effect they had on me and others. I became depressed and along with this came my biggest nightmare, panic attacks. They showed no mercy and struck when I was travelling to and from work as well as when I was in the office.

Things got so bad that I saw my doctor who wisely told me to make changes in my life that would make things easier for me. So I did: I told the bank I would work only four days a week. Secretly I think I was hoping they would say no and then it would push me into doing something else. But they did not, and I became the first person ever to be allowed to do this at the bank where I worked.

Sadly this did not work either; the panic attacks increased and I

xiii

was back to the doctor's and the drawing board. What a wise woman she turned out to be. 'What would make your day happier?' she asked. 'Not having to travel to London each day,' I immediately replied, 'to do a job I hate and to see friends and colleagues who are equally stressed out as me.' 'Then don't,' she promptly said as if she had found the answer to all life's mysteries. I left the surgery with her words ringing in my ears and her encouragement in my heart. Next day I handed in my notice and two weeks later I took a part-time job in a chemist where I stayed quite happily until my eldest son was born.

Over the years following I became a journalist and combined this with having three more children. As I was a 'freelancer' it was not always easy to find work, and so to help pay the bills I took what I thought would be an ideal job for me as a school secretary. And yes, I loved it. The job was varied, interesting and it gave me great satisfaction. The teachers were friendly towards me and so were the children. What I had not reckoned on, though, were Joan and Nora, the other two secretaries.

Both were senior and much older than me. I noticed right from the day I started that they hated children (not ideal when working in a school) and did their utmost to make the lives of those unfortunate enough to cross their paths downright miserable. During my interview one poor nervous child knocked on the office door to say he had forgotten his packed lunch and I nearly fell off the chair when Nora bellowed at him. 'Then you will have to starve! Now get out.' I suppose that should have told me what she was like, but I wanted the job and I was sure that this must just be one of her bad days.

I very quickly learnt that it was not and that you never ever asked how she was or said, 'Good morning' until she was ready to say it to you. Some days I would be ignored completely, never knowing why.

Unwell children hid in my office rather than run the gauntlet with Joan and Nora, and many is the time I have trusted a child who had forgotten his packed lunch to pay for a school dinner the following day and accepted the sick or dental note a day late.

Balancing the books for the school dinner money may seem an easy job but with nearly 2,500 children, some having free lunches, and 40 teachers it was no mean task. Sometimes I would have to work extra hours to find where one lunch had disappeared to that week, because Nora and Joan would insist that there could be no discrepancies even if I offered to put the 40p in. Yet when Nora lost a whole folder containing a large number of postage stamps she replaced these out of her own pocket at great cost rather than tell the head teacher. Gradually the contemptible way they treated the children got to me and I began to dread going into work and listening to the children being shouted at and getting upset.

I could feel myself getting depressed, and then one day I had a panic attack. I remembered the wise words that my doctor had spoken all those years ago and I handed in my notice and left. The headmaster even came to my office twice to ask if I would stay. 'The children like you,' he said. I have to say I hesitated, but he knew the reason why I was leaving and was obviously not able to do anything about it . . . but I could.

The depression gradually lifted as I went back to what I loved, freelance journalist work. I went to college to train as a counsellor and from this I was able to achieve my life-long ambition of becoming an agony aunt. As I said before, I can still remember what it was like to feel depressed and I would not wish this on my worst enemy.

When depression is work-induced there is the added worry that you must have brought it upon yourself because others seem to be coping.

Do not do this to yourself or let anyone else make you feel guilty or inadequate.

If work is piled on to you because your employers want to cut back on staff and save money . . . there is a limit to what one person can physically and mentally cope with . . . it's not your fault.

Neither is it if you are given inadequate training or asked to do things that are not part of your contract, or if new strategies are brought into play because some bright spark has been on a course and wants to implement what they have learnt despite the fact that it is not right for the type of company you are working for.

You have probably picked up this book for your own individual reasons but also because you have realized that work is making you depressed, something perhaps it has never done before. As an agony aunt I have received hundreds of letters over the past few years from readers and listeners who say, 'I used to love my job but now things have changed and I dread going to work.' Employers will often say, 'It's progress. If they can't stand the heat they should get out of the kitchen.' But these people cannot all be wrong despite what employers like to think and say; things have changed in the workplace, and where health is concerned not for the better.

They have introduced computers and new technology at the cost of many people's jobs, and somewhere along the line these machines have become more important than people and their feelings. I hope you will find in this book the sympathy, understanding and encouragement you may need at the moment.

This book is about helping yourself to beat depression and make changes in your working life. It is not just a book to read, it is a workshop also, and I will be asking you to take time to do certain things yourself that I feel may help. You can read it from cover to cover or just dip into the sections you feel comfortable with. Whether you bought, borrowed or had this book given to you the important thing is that you have a copy in your hand, which shows you have taken the first step to changing your working life for the better.

So travel through its pages, and together I am sure we can find a way to lift the depression in the workplace for you.

Kind regards,

Vicky

1

Depressed . . . Not Me!

This is Nick's story just as he told it to me. If you are depressed, or know of someone who is, you might find it strikes a few chords.

I got up for work at 7 o'clock on 6 October and went downstairs to get my wife's breakfast tray ready to take upstairs. I looked at the clock on the microwave cooker and hadn't a clue what '7.44' meant and didn't know what I was doing. The digits changed to 7.45 and I thought, of course, it's a quarter to eight and I am getting my wife's breakfast. I took a tray upstairs to our bedroom where she gets ready for work. I briefly outlined the 'clock' experience then went downstairs.

All went well until 9.15 when my year 7 science group came into the room. I had my planner and my copy of the text book in front of me. The students were almost settled down when suddenly I realized that I didn't know why I was there and what I had to do. I read to myself the first few lines of the lesson I had written and it fell into place that I was going to do an investigation into relative strengths of different tissue papers.

The day went along as planned until about 1.20. My wife had finished taking the register of her form in my biology lab and said to me, 'Are you OK now, Nick?' Something snapped and I said, 'No, I don't think I am,' and walked out of the room with my eyes filling with tears. I went straight to see my head teacher. He was very sympathetic and caring and suggested I went home. My wife's class was taken over by a colleague so that she could go with me.

The next day I saw my doctor and got an appointment to have a blood test done. When I walked home from the surgery I stared at the pavement all the time and even crossed the road to avoid having to meet people I knew. I felt guilty, ashamed and frightened. Guilty because the students at school would suffer in terms of their progress. Ashamed because although I have a good bit of responsibility at work so do many others, and they seemed to cope. I felt frightened because neither my head teacher nor I could find a reason for this happening. All the staff at the school are literally like one happy family, therefore the reason wasn't due to relationships in the staff room. I rarely had discipline problems – certainly no major ones with the students – and my department is quite successful.

The results of the appointment with the doctor was that the blood test was clear and he diagnosed me as suffering from chronic anxiety and depression. The doctor told me at our first meeting that it could take three to six months or even longer for me to recover. I don't think I believed him at the time. I thought that in a couple of weeks I would be OK. But I was wrong, it was to take much longer.

Like many other people Nick's depression came on out of the blue and he couldn't believe what was happening because there seemed to be no reason for it. His whole life was turned upside down. Sadly this happens all the time; even the most cheerful person who no one would ever dream could be depressed can be affected. Sadness and feelings of emptiness intrude into your life, and suddenly there seems no point to anything.

There are many myths about depression and we need to dispel these before we go any further.

- Being 'well off' doesn't protect anyone from being depressed. Film stars, pop idols, MPs, managing directors, titled people, even royalty can become sufferers. Depression affects people from all walks of life.
- Only weak inadequate people get depressed . . . wrong! Depression is a common illness which affects one in four of us at some stage in our lives.
- Once depressed, always depressed . . . wrong! Like most other illnesses it can be treated successfully.
- Depression is not a proper illness . . . wrong! It is as much an illness as diabetes or heart disease.
- If you take antidepressants you will be hooked for life . . . wrong! You won't become dependent on antidepressants. People often confuse these with tranquillizers, which can be addictive.
- Only women get depressed . . . wrong! Although it is likely that at some point in their lives one in five women will get depressed, one in ten men also suffers with depression, and at any one time one in every twenty adults is experiencing a serious bout of

depression. It is estimated that every year three out of ten people at work will have mental health problems, with depression being top of the list.

So, you see, you are not alone. It is a real illness, there is nothing to be ashamed of and you will get better.

Although depression can come on suddenly, for many people it is a far more gradual process, which makes it harder to recognize. Other people, because of the stigma attached to depression, refuse to recognize it or admit to anyone that they could possibly be depressed.

Let us now look at the symptoms of depression. Most of us will have had days when we feel fed up or down in the dumps, sometimes without any major reason but because we feel sad, tired, disappointed, bored or the weather is bad. Other times things happen in our lives such as family problems, illness and money worries that make us feel miserable and low, but after a while these feelings pass and life gets back to normal. But sometimes these sad and miserable feelings remain, and that is when we become depressed. To help you decide whether you are suffering with depression, fill in the following checklist.

Signs of depression

Please tick in the appropriate box in Figure 1.

Figure 1

		Yes	No
1	Do you feel there is nothing to look forward to?	☐	☐
2	Do you feel down and tearful?	☐	☐
3	Have you noticed a change in your sleep pattern, sleeping too much or too little?	☐	☐
4	Have you lost interest in eating or started over-eating?	☐	☐
5	Do you feel life is pointless?	☐	☐
6	Are you feeling tired all the time?	☐	☐
7	Do you feel guilty about things?	☐	☐
8	Are you having difficulty concentrating and becoming forgetful?	☐	☐
9	Have you become confused?	☐	☐
10	Have you lost interest in sex?	☐	☐
11	Are you agitated?	☐	☐
12	Do you have overwhelming feelings of anxiety?	☐	☐
13	Are you losing confidence in yourself?	☐	☐
14	Do you get irritable or angry more often than you used to?	☐	☐
15	Do you feel scared about the way you feel?	☐	☐

If you have ticked four or more Yes boxes and have felt this way for more than three weeks go and see your doctor.

Quite a number of people who suffer with depression may also suffer physical symptoms such as headaches, palpitations, upset stomach, nausea and aching limbs, but not everyone does.

One of the biggest hurdles sufferers of depression have to overcome is admitting to themselves that they are depressed. It is something that happens to other people, not themselves. Others genuinely don't recognize that they are depressed.

Following a change of job Hugh found himself suffering with depression. To begin with he had looked forward to a new post with positive relief that he had left behind a bullying employer, and had high expectations of this new opportunity which lay before him. He admits he was still harbouring anger over his previous job and the way he was treated and was finding it difficult to forget this. Things however didn't go as he expected with his new job. The harder he tried to fit in the more things seemed to fall apart. His manager was very tolerant and uncritical, although some of his colleagues were not. He couldn't reach the high standards he set himself and was constantly worried about what his colleagues thought of him. He became anxious, stressed and miserable and this led to high blood pressure, which his doctor tried treating but with little success. His doctor asked if he was feeling depressed and he denied it – not because he was hiding anything but because he truly did not recognize his sad feelings as being depression. He never discussed these feelings with his GP because he felt his physical ones were more important. Eventually he went to the hospital for a check-up as the blood pressure had become worse and they could find no obvious reason for this. He told himself it was just anxiety, but as a precaution the hospital asked him to stay in overnight so that they could keep an eye on him. During this time he started to feel that the nursing staff were uncomfortable with his presence, even hostile towards him. When he left next day his mood was very low and he went back to see his GP because he was scared at the depths of despair he was sinking into.

His doctor diagnosed depression, which he had long suspected but which Hugh had not recognized. Over the coming months, with the help of a conscientious doctor and good friends, his depression lifted and his blood pressure went back to normal.

Hugh genuinely didn't recognize that he was depressed, unlike

Tanya, who did but was scared to let anyone know.

Tanya worked as a bus conductress which meant lots of standing and being jogged around – something her waterworks couldn't cope with. On several occasions she had found herself wanting to spend a penny with a long part of the journey still ahead of her. Although there were toilets along the route Tanya found it embarrassing to ask the driver to stop and to leave the bus with a load of passengers watching her disappearing into a toilet. On one occasion the bus driver had got irritated with her; on another she used a coin electrically operated toilet booth and several passengers had jokingly made comments about what might have happened to them if the door hadn't opened and she had got stuck in there. Although she laughed, inside she was mortified. After this she would worry herself sick in case the need to go to the toilet arose again. She wouldn't eat or drink before her shift or in breaks and would go to the toilet several times before boarding the bus.

She knew this was affecting her mental and physical health; she recognized the feeling of depression but couldn't bring herself to say anything to anyone or ask for help. Eventually she was forced to see her doctor with kidney and urinary problems brought on by lack of fluids. She broke down and told her doctor how it had come about and how depressed she was.

Although Tanya never returned to being a bus conductress her employers were far more understanding than she had ever given them credit for. She now has an administrative job at the bus station and has trained to become their first-aid officer.

Getting help

Both of these case histories show how important it is to seek help as quickly as you can and to tell people how you are feeling. Hugh could have been helped earlier if he had told the doctor how he was feeling emotionally as well as physically. In Tanya's case, embarrassment stopped her getting help and caused her painful physical symptoms, some of which could have a lasting effect.

Understanding that depression is an illness and not a weakness is something I shall be reminding you of all through this book. It is nothing for you to be ashamed of, and just like any other illness it can be cured so long as you seek help. Apart from your doctor, your family and friends can play an important role in your recovery. Your depression will certainly show you who your real friends are.

Mahatma Gandhi is quoted as saying, 'The test of friendship is assistance in adversity and that, too, unconditional assistance.'

You will learn how true this saying is. Some friends who you felt were very loyal won't be able to help because of their fears relating to any kind of mental illness. It's the true friends who try to understand who will offer you a lifeline during periods of depression. They listen, sympathize, encourage and are an important link with the way you used to be in happier days and the way it could be again. Don't push them away or turn your back on them. It's easy to do so when you feel everyone is against you or doesn't understand how you feel. There is an old saying, 'A friend in need is a friend indeed' and none so much as when you are feeling depressed and alone.

Most of us will suffer some kind of physical pain and can envisage the pain associated with other illnesses, but with mental illness it is completely different. You can't begin to imagine what it is like to be so mentally low that you can't face the day, make decisions or work unless you have been through it yourself. In fact many people are very ignorant and thoughtless when it comes to dealing with someone who is depressed.

They say things they wouldn't dream of saying to someone who was well. Maisie, a nurse, became depressed when she was 26. She left the stressful job in the maternity unit where she had worked for three years and took up a part-time care assistant role and some voluntary work. She told me how deflated she would feel when someone said to her, 'Why can't you think positive and get yourself a proper job, love!' Someone else said, 'Jean's husband died last year but she hasn't given up on her life or sat around feeling sorry for herself. You ought to get out more like she does.' When she made the mistake of revealing she had been in hospital for depression, someone stupidly said, 'You wouldn't catch me in a place like that.' As if Maisie had been given the choice in the first place!

The environment and people you work with can cause depression and have an influence on the way you cope with it and how soon you recover.

Shop-floor worker Arthur described his place of work as Dickensian. It was drab, dull, badly lit and oily. He said the fact that his home environment was sparkling clean and comfortable, and so were the places where he socialized with his wife, made the work environment seem worse when he returned each day.

During his eight-hour shift he said he was faced with degrading shop-floor language, pornographic calendars and pictures on the walls, dirty toilets, bad manners from other workers and pressure from supervisors and management. Add to this the dirt, grime and smells of the metal components and he felt it was little wonder that he became depressed or had any other choice than to leave the 'Oliver Twist' environment. Like many others he found it impossible to change the ways things were, but fortunately he managed to take control of his life and make the decision to leave. Far too many people are trapped in similar depressing circumstances and don't know what to do.

If you feel this is happening to you, ask if you are being fair to yourself. Are you allowing others to decide your fate and treat you badly? Look at your options. You can complain about the working conditions, try to alter them yourself or decide to look for somewhere else to work. Challenge mean or sarcastic colleagues: they are less likely to have a go at you in the future if you do so.

The hardest part of becoming depressed is admitting to yourself that you are ill. Although for most people it is a very gradual process, Nick at the beginning of our chapter found it a frightening and dramatic experience. I spoke to him the week I finished this book and he told me that it had taken eight months before he had been able to return to teaching. Although he sometimes panics about things, in the main he is now coping very well. The children at the school where he works are all very supportive, as well as the staff. He gave me the following message to pass on to readers of this book.

'Whatever you do, don't be afraid to talk about your depression and hang on in there, because things do get better.'

Questions and answers

Q I am in a dreadful state. Life doesn't seem worth living any more. My job has been down-graded and I now have to report to a young girl who I trained for her job a couple of years ago. I know I am depressed but I can't go to see my doctor as I need a reference from him for a voluntary job that I want to do and if he knows I am depressed he might not feel inclined to give me a reference if he thought I was cracking up. I talk to friends about my depression and this helps me to feel better.

A Far from branding you as inadequate I am sure your doctor would be impressed that, despite your depression, you are making plans and taking on a new role. That shows someone capable of overcoming depression even though they may need a little help from him along the way. Talking about your feelings is good but remember you have to give to receive, so always find time to enquire how your friends are rather than always talking about yourself.

Q I have always had a moan to a friend at work about pay and conditions and other things but was shocked when she suggested out of the blue that I might be depressed. Of course I denied it, but when she pointed out that I had burst into tears on several occasions and didn't seem to be able to concentrate like I used to her words struck home. I never told her but I did go to see my doctor who said it was all part and parcel of the menopause, not depression. I thankfully accepted this, but three months on I am finding it very difficult to motivate myself at work and I dread going in each day. Even worse, I avoid getting into conversation now with my friend for fear that she will mention depression again, but I also fear that I might be suffering with this.

A Depression and the menopause sometimes go hand in hand so go back to your doctor and explain how you feel. I know you said you moan about work but do be sure there is nothing in your home life that could be also contributing to your depression. It would also be very sad to give up on your friend; what she said was out of concern for you, not to put you down.

Q I became depressed and with a lot of effort did what I thought were the right things. I saw my GP, I got counselling and sought help from my departmental head. So why do people treat me as if I haven't got an ounce of common sense in my head, Vicky? I am fed up with people talking about me as if I had suddenly gone deaf and being left out of things because I might be an embarrassment to them. Where have I gone wrong?

A You haven't gone wrong, in fact you seem to have gone to great lengths to put yourself back on track. There is really no accounting for some folks, they lump all mental illness together without bothering to try to understand that depression makes you feel sad but it doesn't take away all your faculties. Neither does it stop you from wanting to be treated by friends in the same way as you always did. Perhaps a few gentle reminders wouldn't go amiss, and it might also make them feel more comfortable.

2

The Effect of Depression on Work and Home

A question you have to ask yourself is whether your work is making you depressed or whether depression is having an effect on your work. You may think this is rather a strange question to ask, but it isn't. Finding out what is contributing to your depression is a very important factor.

Lots of people say they are depressed over their job, but if you question them about their home or personal lives you might find the reason for their depression has nothing to do with work. They are depressed for other reasons but their sad feelings spill over into their working lives, making it difficult for them to distinguish just where their depressed feelings originate. Sometimes it feels safer to use the workplace as a hook rather than having to accept the painful fact that the problem lies closer to home.

Let's look at two case histories and compare them.

Our first one is about James who is 27 and married to Karen. James was orphaned at 12 when his parents were killed in a road accident, and was brought up by foster-parents who were very kind to him. Despite this he missed the family life he used to have and the one thing he wanted more than anything was to marry and have children of his own.

He met Karen when he was at university. They both went on to become teachers, and then married. Karen was happy to have children but was unable to conceive. Three years and many tests later James was told that the problem lay with him and it was unlikely he would ever be able to father a child. Artificial insemination by donor was suggested but James quickly rejected this and was extremely upset when he realized Karen thought it was an option they should consider.

It was like a stake driven between them. James felt useless, unmanly and angry that Karen could even think about having a child by another man. It would be her child but nothing whatsoever to do with him. Karen was unhappy, confused and felt James was punishing her all the time because he couldn't cope with being the one with the fertility problem.

In between the arguments were long silences, often for days or weeks. James was teaching at a primary school and when he became depressed he started to blame his job. He said teaching was rubbish and that other members of staff put upon him, and he blamed parents for anything that went wrong in the classroom. When one child wasn't paying attention and kept making mistakes he ranted on for hours to Karen about parents who let their children get away with anything, and this in turn caused problems with him in the class. A couple of years previously James would have sat down with the child and asked if anything was wrong. If he had done so on this occasion he would have found out that her granddad had died and that at six she didn't understand what death was all about and was worried that her granddad hadn't gone to heaven.

James's attitude towards other staff, not to mention his pupils, changed rapidly as he became more depressed, and this didn't go unnoticed by the head teacher. He called James in and asked him if anything was wrong. 'Wrong?' James said exasperatedly, 'Everything is wrong. This job is making me ill.'

The head teacher was surprised at this because nothing had changed very much over the past few years. Class sizes were much the same. James hadn't been given any extra responsibilities and he had always got on well with other members of staff.

The following term James was worse and complaints were made by the parents about him after a parents' evening. Comments such as uninterested, irritable, cold, out of touch, rude, brusque were used to describe him, with each saying they were unhappy for their children to be taught by him any longer. The head knew that James was suffering with depression, and although he had tried to be supportive he felt he had no alternative but to insist that James saw his doctor and if necessary took sick leave until he was better. Reluctantly James agreed, saw his doctor and told him his job was the cause of his depression. He started taking antidepressants, but although his depression got a bit better his feelings of anger and resentment did not improve. He wasn't doing the job that he had blamed for the depression any longer, as he decided to give up teaching, yet he still felt depressed. He went to work in his foster-father's garden centre, a job he enjoyed, but he felt no better. Eventually his doctor arranged for him to have counselling, and through this he was helped to accept that the real reason for his depression was his inability to father a child and his battered self-esteem when his wife suggested she would be willing to have another man's child by artificial insemination.

Sadly, James and Karen split up and are divorcing. James has accepted that he has a problem but he hopes one day he will be able to overcome this and meet someone else and have the children he wants.

James's strong desire to father children isn't likely to change, but if he could have realized his depression was caused by this and not by his work he might still be doing the teaching job that he is good at, and maybe his marriage would not have ended in divorce.

Our second case history is about Peggy, who became depressed and blamed her husband for it when in fact it was the poor working conditions at the breaker's yard where she worked that were at the root of her problem.

Peggy worked in a Portakabin which was cold, dingily lit and stank of stale cigarettes as the lads who worked in the yard and many of the customers would smoke in there. The toilet facilities were appalling and were really only meant for the men, and so Peggy would have to get in her car and drive down to the local supermarket to use their toilets instead.

Because Peggy had wanted to return to work for ages and had difficulty in getting a job, subconsciously she could not bear to say or do anything that would affect it. She took her bad moods out on her husband and was convinced that he was the one that was making her depressed. It was only when her grown-up children took her to task over the way she was treating their dad that she agreed to see her doctor and take medication. A few weeks later Peggy took a good look around herself when she was at work and didn't like what she saw. She decided to leave her job and take a couple of months off to see if the medication would help her overcome the terrible feelings of depression which she was suffering. It took much longer than two months, but gradually Peggy recovered and realized that her husband hadn't contributed to her illness. It was the poor working conditions and her expectations of herself that had made her depressed.

If you are depressed at work it is important to try and focus on what is causing the depression. To help you do this I would like you to do a simple 'self-assessment chart' like Figures 2 and 3 below.

Read the questions carefully before answering them. Make sure you are honest with your answers. It is easy to think we are making ourselves safe, but the truth is that unless you can recognize and face up to what is causing the problems they hang around, and so does the depression.

As with any of the things that I ask you to do in this book, if you find this exercise difficult or painful leave it for a couple of weeks and then try again. If you can only answer a few of the questions each time then that's fine.

Tick either yes or no to each of the questions, and this will help you to clarify in your mind what may be triggering your depression.

Once you have done this exercise you will be able to compare your working life with your personal one and see what areas could be contributing to your depression. You may find there are things both at work and at home that are causing you to be unhappy, and this is quite normal. The important thing is to see what you can change and what you may have to accept. No one is asking you to make radical changes in your life, but it is important to recognize problem areas: just doing this is often the first step to taking charge of your life rather than it taking control of you.

Most workplaces have changed a lot over the past few years. Redundancies have taken their toll. New technology may have brought improvements to industry, business and commerce but it has also put a lot of pressure and stress on workers. More is expected of them in the way of both expertise and output. It is no wonder that it has brought about fear and depression for many people.

Being depressed makes people behave uncharacteristically both in their lives at home and in their relationships at work. Even though you may be able to identify causes for your depression it won't stop it affecting all areas of your life. At times your family will be under as much of a strain as you are. It's not easy being a carer, and although they may not always be able to cope with your depression it won't be because they don't care. The person they used to know has temporarily been replaced by someone who is sad, unable to concentrate or enjoy anything and who worries yet can't talk about things. This isn't your fault or theirs and there is no need to feel

Figure 2

Work

	Yes	No
1 Are you happy in your job?	☐	☐
2 Do you look forward to going to work?	☐	☐
3 Do you dread going to work?	☐	☐
4 Do you get on with your colleagues?	☐	☐
5 Have there been changes at work?	☐	☐
6 Do you dislike any of the changes?	☐	☐
7 Is your job secure?	☐	☐
8 Do you fear redundancy?	☐	☐
9 Are you happy with your salary?	☐	☐
10 Is the work repetitive?	☐	☐
11 Are you bored with your job?	☐	☐
12 Do you want more variety in your work?	☐	☐
13 Do you get on with your manager/supervisor?	☐	☐
14 Is there a chance of promotion?	☐	☐
15 Would you want promotion?	☐	☐
16 Is the environment you work in good?	☐	☐
17 Do you feel too much is expected of you?	☐	☐
18 Do you need more training in technology?	☐	☐
19 Do you feel a victim at work?	☐	☐
20 Would you change jobs if you had the chance?	☐	☐

Figure 3

Personal life

	Yes	No
1 Do you have a partner?	☐	☐
2 If yes are you happy with them?	☐	☐
3 Do you argue with your partner?	☐	☐
4 Are the arguments usually about the same thing?	☐	☐
5 Have you tried to resolve any differences?	☐	☐
6 Do you have financial problems?	☐	☐
7 Do you have any family conflicts?	☐	☐
8 Do you have to look after elderly relatives or dependants?	☐	☐
9 Are your children a source of worry?	☐	☐
10 Have you been unable to start a family?	☐	☐
11 Do you like where you live?	☐	☐
12 If you do not have a partner are you lonely?	☐	☐
13 Do you want to meet someone?	☐	☐
14 Are you making an effort to meet someone?	☐	☐
15 Are you happy with your sex life?	☐	☐
16 Is your partner happy sexually?	☐	☐
17 If you are gay do people know?	☐	☐
18 If you are gay and married do you feel trapped?	☐	☐
19 Do you feel you should be making more of an effort with your relationship?	☐	☐
20 Have you ever thought of leaving your partner?	☐	☐

guilty. This is an illness just like any other and the prospect of recovery is very good.

In the workplace depression has a marked influence on how sufferers interact with people they come in contact with both face to face and on the phone. Let's look at the practical side first. If you are depressed and working a lot of the time on the phone, you may not realize it but your voice and how you come over to customers or clients may reflect the way you feel. So it is important that you recognize this and make a conscious effort to lift your voice so that it continues to sound pleasant to anyone who talks to you on the phone.

Emily worked for the tele-sales department of a local newspaper for five years and had always come close to the top of the sales figures in her department. When certain new incentives were brought in she began to feel the strain. One of the managers came up with the idea of putting an alarm clock in a box each day and whoever had just sold advertising space when the alarm went off got a bonus or a gift. The clock was reset by the manager twice a day. It really was down to luck, and although Emily knew this and was still selling plenty of ad-space she found after a month that she was one of the few who hadn't won anything. It had been meant as a bit of fun as well as an incentive to keep them all working but Emily saw it as pressure and failure. Gradually she lost interest in the work and dreaded going in some days. She became quiet and withdrawn and depressed. Her voice became duller and uninterested and lacked enthusiasm. Her sales figures fell. Fortunately for Emily, her manager noticed a change in her and took her to one side to talk things through. Emily told him how she felt and her manager told her he was going to transfer her for three months to work on admin and subbing so that she didn't feel under pressure. He said she should see this as a long overdue opportunity to learn new skills and further her career. This is what he told the other tele-sales staff who asked why Emily was moving. He addressed a difficult situation with no embarrassment to Emily. When I met her she told me her ambition is to be Ad. Manager.

The same applies to any letters, faxes or e-mails that you send. Be aware that your depressed feelings may affect the wording, so re-read before sending and if in doubt ask someone who you work with and trust to check the letter. Most people spend up to a third of their lives at work, and this is a long time to have to get through when you are feeling depressed. No wonder many have to take time off. It is especially difficult if you feel work colleagues don't understand or you have tried to keep your depression a secret. Later on in the book we shall look in more detail at whether or not to tell your employer or colleagues that you are depressed, but for the purpose of this chapter I think it is important to work out who you can trust, and tell them as early on in your illness as you can how you are feeling. By 'trust' I mean someone who will be supportive without broadcasting it to everyone else you work with. Just knowing there is someone at work who understands will make all the difference and may stop your depression from getting worse.

Questions and answers

Q Following several bouts of depression my husband asked me for a divorce. I was stunned and at once suspected there was someone else. He assured me there wasn't but said he thought I was the cause of his depression because I bored him. He was convinced that once we split up his depression would miraculously disappear, but of course it didn't. Six months on from the divorce he is still as depressed as ever. I met someone who works with him who said everyone was shocked when he told them of our divorce. They told me he had been as miserable as sin at work long before we split, and that it was because he had been passed over for promotion when he had been convinced it was in the bag this time. I didn't know anything about this interview but he has been short-listed several times and never got any of the jobs. His sister tells me his depression is just as bad. I wouldn't have him back now for love nor money, but I wonder if I spoke to him if he would admit that it isn't my fault that he is depressed. It hurts a lot to know that he thinks this.

A Of course it hurts, but all the time he is depressed it is unlikely that he will be willing to discuss what has happened, let alone admit he is wrong. To do so would mean he would have to face up to the truth that he is failing to get promotion at work and this hurts him. Maybe he felt you would think badly of him and to protect himself he made the decision to end your marriage. Believe me, you do not need any admissions on his part to make you feel better. You know that he made this decision while he was ill and he may even be regretting this now. You have to look after yourself and not let what he says eat away at you. He has to face up to the reality of what is causing his depression but only he can do this, and in his own good time.

Q   A friend at work is suffering with depression and has confided in me that her husband is having an affair. He is aware that she knows but refuses to give up the other woman. She isn't sleeping or eating and looks dreadful; she is tired when she gets into work and is finding it hard to concentrate. People are beginning to notice because she is making silly mistakes. Our manager asked her if there was anything wrong, but she said there wasn't because she was ashamed of what is going on in her life. I have been checking her work so that she doesn't get into trouble but I am falling behind with my own and comments have been made to me about this. I don't want to let my friend down and I am worried about her, but this is having an effect on my work as well.

A   She is a lucky lady to have such a good friend as you, but apart from listening when she needs to talk there isn't anything else that you can do. Without betraying her confidence you can't afford to jeopardize your job. Next time you talk suggest that she goes for counselling at Relate. If her husband won't go with her then they will see her on her own. She desperately needs her confidence boosting. At the moment knowing her husband is having sex elsewhere must be hacking away all her self-esteem. Relate helps couples to separate as amicably as possible as well as staying together. You can play an important part in this, alongside counselling, by helping her to realize that she does not have to remain a victim in this marriage and that maybe confiding in her manager might just take the pressure off her and help her depression.

Q   My name is Keith and I know what I am doing is unfair to everyone but I don't know how to put things right. I married my wife 22 years ago knowing I was gay. She wanted a family, but I refused because I had always had the fear that I might not be able to stay with her feeling the way I do. I didn't marry until I was 27 and only then because my mother found out I was in a gay relationship and thought marriage would cure me. So I married Maria, the

19

daughter of my mother's friend, who was 35. Since we married I have been faithful and she doesn't know that I am gay. Sex was infrequent to start with and then became non-existent after two years. She has never complained about this and we now have separate rooms. Over the last year or so I have become very frustrated with my life and depressed. I work as a taxi driver for a company and have hours each day sitting in the cab just going over everything in my mind. I am irritated with passengers who seem to whine about everything and my mind always seems to be on my problems. The crunch came this week when my boss called me in and said he was getting complaints from customers about me being rude and aggressive. I made excuses but I know what he says is true. I bring my problems to work because there is no way to resolve them at home.

A   Listen Keith . . . you may well have boxed yourself into a corner but if you can pluck up the courage and be honest with your wife there will be a way out. Many men have found themselves in your situation. Twenty years ago it was hard to admit to being gay, and like you lots of men got pushed into marriage by well-meaning parents in an attempt to cure them. You know and I know that this doesn't work. Maybe Maria is more aware of your situation than you give her credit for. She certainly deserves the truth and the opportunity to decide what she wants for the rest of her life and to be happy. She may decide it is time to part, leaving you to make the relationship you want, or she may want to stay providing any relationship you have is discreet and doesn't hurt her. Either way, Keith, you need to sort this out. You can't afford to let the depression caused in your personal life affect your concentration when driving. See your GP and think hard about 'coming out'. You know it makes sense.

3

No Longer Needed

Apart from the obvious financial rewards, being employed can give people status, self-esteem, confidence in their ability, friends and colleagues and a purpose to their day. Take this away and it can lead to a lack of confidence and depression. It's one of the things people who retire have to cope with once the first flush of enjoying having time to themselves after years of working has passed; they often find that time hangs heavy on their hands. It is even harder when redundancy or downsizing strikes out of the blue and you lose your job.

It was a lovely summer's day when Duncan set off for work, unaware that his whole life was to be turned upside down. When he travelled to the city his only thoughts were that this time next week he would be lying on a beach with his family when he took his annual leave. Duncan always thought his job was secure so it came as a dreadful shock when he was called in by the manager and told he was redundant.

Because he worked with computer programmes he was told to clear his desk and leave immediately. After 23 years he could hardly believe this was happening to him. Less than an hour after arriving at work he was sitting in his car too stunned to drive home.

His bank account would be swelled by the redundancy money and he thought he remembered the manager had told him his salary for that month plus holiday pay would also be paid in. Money wouldn't be a problem, but how could he tell Mary and the children that he had lost his job?

Eight hours later Duncan arrived home, ate his meal, had a bath and went to bed saying he had a headache. He could not bring himself to tell them that he no longer had a job.

During the night he lay awake worrying about what to do. Eventually he convinced himself that he could get another job and that there would be no need to worry Mary until he had sorted things out. He could use his redundancy money to live on.

So that day and for the next three months he left the house as usual and went and spent the day in the libary, writing letters or reading the situations vacant columns in the newspapers. He confided only in his best friend, who reluctantly agreed that he could use his address for mail to be forwarded to and for telephone messages.

Fortunately his wife had never telephoned him at work as the bank did not encourage personal calls, and so he had no worries there. Although there were jobs he could have taken there was nothing that matched the salary or status that the bank job had given him. Trying to get through each day and the deception was even more tiring than going to work, and gradually he found himself getting more and more depressed. Eventually things came to a head when his wife got angry because she said he was always moody and short-tempered with her and the children. Much to her horror he broke down and told her what had been going on.

It was shortly after this that he came to me for counselling, as his wife had told him she couldn't stay with someone who was capable of living a lie. Reluctantly she agreed to come with him. Duncan told us he felt he had let his family down by losing his job. This reduced Mary to tears, and over the coming weeks she came to understand that maybe she contributed as much as Duncan to the lack of communication between them because she was very orderly, liked everything in its right place and did not like anything to upset her. She was, however, keen to reassure Duncan that it was not his fault that he had lost his job and that although she hated the deceit she could understand how it had undermined his self-esteem.

Eventually Duncan returned to work, this time as a wages cashier for a local factory. He still had a way to go in building up his confidence, but at least he and Mary were still together and I don't think he will need to lie to her again.

There is no getting away from the fact that being made redundant is a form of rejection and one that strikes at the heart of a person's self-esteem. If you have been unhappy at work, then after the initial shock it can be a blessing in disguise and eventually seen as a chance to make a fresh start. If on the other hand you always enjoyed your work and this came out of the blue, it will be a great shock and one that may be hard to recover from.

It's when this happens that the person retreats into themselves and becomes depressed. All kinds of emotions come into play and confidence in all areas of their life plummets. What you have to hang on to is that it's not your fault, so stop punishing yourself with guilt and insecurities.

When you work for someone other than yourself you are handing over to them the responsibility to keep you employed. You contribute by working to the running of the company but you don't make the decisions – the ultimate ones lie with the management, and people are made redundant for financial reasons within the company. It is just that you were in the wrong place at the wrong time.

There has been a move over the last few years towards downsizing and imaging in many companies. Downsizing is where companies get rid of a percentage of their staff and expect the rest of the employees to take on the extra work as well as what they were doing already. This is in contrast to redundancy, when often a job is dispensed with altogether.

Some of the people who lose their jobs are given sideways or downwards moves to jobs that are repetitive, boring and lacking in challenge. Often this can involve fewer hours and less money; some even manage to downgrade people and still expect the same work done.

Mandy was one of two restaurant managers who lost her job when the chain decided that they would have a general manager who would oversee both outlets, saving them almost two-thirds of what they had been paying Mandy and her colleague at the other restaurant. Her salary was cut, her title was taken away from her and yet she was still doing exactly the same work and taking the same responsibilities each day but getting paid less.

The new general manager floated in from time to time, treating her like a waitress, and there was no one she could talk to about the way she was being treated. She was part-time, had no contract and was told if she didn't like it she could leave. Like many others she became disillusioned and depressed, lacking in self-confidence. Eventually she did leave, which was probably what they wanted in the first place.

In the case of both Duncan and Mandy their situations were completely out of their control; they had done their jobs well and to the best of their ability. Even though they were assets to the

23

companies they worked for, money was more important to their employers, and this appears to be so with many companies today.

If you find yourself in this situation it's very important that right from the start you get it fixed very firmly in your mind that what has happened is not your fault and in no way reflects on your work. These are decisions made by those higher up who don't see their workers as people with feelings. Profit is first and foremost in their minds, and so long as their jobs are secure they do what it takes to ensure the company grows.

Imaging is where work is sent abroad to be done by people who will do it for far less money, and this is becoming a common practice with many larger companies who can see the advantages of saving money in this way. With most work being done on computers in business today it means that it can be carried out from a terminal in a poorer country such as India just as easily as in London, Paris or New York.

Downsizing is just another word for cutback, and it can cause just as much stress for those who keep their jobs as those who don't. Quite often when people lose their job it is not because it has ceased to exist; the work they did is still there but others have to absorb this workload along with the work they already have, so the companies save money at the expense of the staff being stretched to the limit.

Some time ago when I was talking about depression in the workplace at a conference I met a lady called Ann who worked for Social Services. She told me she had held her present position for 19 years, and although the work had always been stressful she enjoyed it. Ten months before, two of her colleagues who did a job share had been made redundant and she had been given their work, which meant her workload doubled overnight. Although relieved that she had kept her job she was worried as to how she was going to cope with this extra burden.

It soon became apparent Ann couldn't cope. Jobs were being left half done, others not touched. She went to see her line manager hoping that a solution to help her could be found; instead she was told other members of staff were coping with extra work and she needed to get herself better organized.

With these words stinging in her ears she muddled through for another few weeks, often working from seven in the morning until nine at night in a vain attempt to clear the workload.

With her personal assessment due Ann became more and more worried, often not sleeping for nights on end. She knew it was not just the extra work that wasn't getting done, the whole of her workload was being affected. At her assessment she was told they were disappointed in her work and because of this she would have to be assessed again in two months. With this hanging over her head she became agitated and depressed, until eventually she had to go and see her doctor because she felt so ill. She was immediately signed off sick, and when I met her she was still at home. She told me she had written to her employers stating that she felt it was unreasonable to expect one person to do the work that had originally been two full-time jobs being done by three people. The company never replied to her comments; they just sent an acknowledgement of her sickness certificate.

She had no idea who was doing the work while she was away but was dreading the day when she would have to return. At 54 with only six years left before she retired she did not think she could look for another job and felt very trapped; the best she thought she could hope for was early retirement on the grounds of ill health, and eventually she wrote to me saying there was a strong possibility that this was going to happen.

It is such a shame that she was ever put into this dreadful situation, because what could have been a productive and happy last six years of her working life has been taken away from her and replaced with despair, depression, disappointment and lack of self-confidence.

Richard is another victim of the ripples downsizing can cause. As the manager of a department in a large store he found himself faced with having to make two out of four of his assistants redundant. All had been there over 15 years, one of them 25. He wrestled for days over who should go and who should stay. Telling two of his employees that they had lost their job was a real ordeal for Richard and he felt he had let his colleagues down, even though he had only done what the management had told him to.

Running the department with half of the staff proved very difficult for everyone but even more so for Richard, who was riddled with guilt. With a sick wife and a handicapped son to look after he was constantly worried that his job might be the next one to go. He became depressed and tried to hide it, but the store manager had noticed a change in him and asked to see him.

Fortunately for Richard this was to be the turning point in his depression, because the store manager had suffered with depression himself some years previously and told Richard nothing was worth getting yourself ill over.

He told him to take two weeks off sick and that during this time he would try and find a way of easing the workload in his department. A week later Richard received a call telling him that a part-time assistant had been employed to work on Thursdays, Fridays and Saturdays, which were the busiest days. It did not make up for the loss of two full-timers, but knowing that his boss understood and had done what he could to help made all the difference to Richard and the other staff.

Many of the people who retain their jobs after others have lost theirs are affected very badly by what has happened. For some, one of the biggest worries is that it will be their turn next, while others feel guilty because they still have their jobs when their friends have not. When you spend at least a third of your life at work it is only natural that friendships are formed. These are threatened when jobs are lost. The one who has lost their job may feel resentful and angry, and this is often transferred on to their friend who is left behind. It is therefore very important that a distinct line is drawn between what has happened and friendship. If you have lost your job, ask yourself how many friends you have that you can afford to lose those you had at work over something that is beyond their control. They will be concerned for you, not laughing behind your back, so keep in touch, and do not let anyone take your friendships away.

The same goes for those who still have their jobs: keep in touch, be sympathetic, but try to move your friendship on to a different level, one that has nothing to do with work. If you can do this you will both benefit.

Changing things

We have looked at some of the problems that cause depression at work, and now it is time to see what can be done to try and change the situation. You cannot force employers to keep on staff, but what you can do is look after your own interests. If you are being asked, like Ann, to do the work of two people, register your concern at the outset. Remind your employer that the quality of work is as important as the quantity, and that a point is reached when this is jeopardized. The chances are you will be told to 'see how things go' as a brush-off. If this happens start keeping a 'time management chart' where you list down each hour what you have done. Hearing the words 'time management' might make you cringe, especially if you have been made to do this in the past by your company to see if you are working to your full potential, or 'to speed', as they often say. Do not let this put you off; use it to your own advantage. Yes, it can be a bit tedious, but once you get into the habit it will only take a few moments. Also keep a 'day book' and make a list each day of key tasks and lesser ones. At the end of each day, mark off what you have achieved and bring forward in red what you have not. Concentrate each time on the jobs in hand and do not worry about the next until you start it. By doing this you will be able to see for yourself how much work you are getting through each day and what the backlog is. Don't make yourself ill with worry trying to get it all done. By organizing what you can do you will lessen the chance of becoming depressed. At the end of a couple of months ask to see your manager again and show your records. They may not be happy that you are 'rocking the boat', but at least they will have hard evidence in front of them that you are working to the best of your ability and that it is not possible for you to soak up the work of another full-time person who has left.

The alternative is to muddle through and achieve very little, get yourself into a state and become depressed. Most depressed feelings to do with the workplace are brought about by changes that are made beyond the control of the employees. They are made to feel as if they do not count, that they are dispensable and of no value to anyone, including their family.

If you feel like this you may find the 'dumping box' exercise helps. Find a box with a lid and sit quietly with this in front of you. Also have to hand a pen and some paper cut into small squares. Dimming the lights and having gentle soft music playing in the background may also help you to relax. Look at the box: this is where you are going to dump all the feelings that are making you feel depressed. It is yours to do with as you wish, no one else need know about it.

As you sit and stare at the box let your mind wander over feelings that are making you unhappy. Anger, resentment or abandonment may be among the first to surface, but whatever the feeling, slowly reach for the pen and paper and write either a word or a single statement. What you put, however strongly, does not matter. Then take off the lid and place the paper inside the box and tell yourself you are dealing with the emotion by acknowledging it, then dumping it.

This exercise is about owning up to certain feelings and accepting them. Only place in the box feelings that you are ready to get rid of, but remember, you can always take them out again for an airing whenever you want.

One person I know who did this put his boss's name on a piece of paper because he was so angry with the way he had treated him when he became depressed. Instead of trying to understand, he had called Colin a skiver and said his depression was self-induced. Colin found it very therapeutic to shut his boss away in the box, but from time to time he would bring out the piece of paper with his boss's name on it and tear it up into little pieces. He always wrote out another, but he said it gave him great satisfaction to do this rather than be aggressive to the man he still had to work for.

It is difficult to change an employer's uncaring attitude alone, but collectively, if you can get together with other workmates, it can be done.

Miriam did this when downsizing was about to take place in her office. As departmental supervisor she was told she had to decide which people would stay and go. Faced with tough decisions that would leave her and a few others having to cope with a huge increase in workload, Miriam instead called a meeting of all the staff in her department to discuss the matter.

Two people asked if they could take early retirement as they were already suffering with depression. This would, they said, be better than forcing other people to leave. The rest agreed they would rather take a small decrease in their salary each week and keep their jobs rather than be forced out.

They put together a proposal to the management, who were stunned when they received it but later agreed on the grounds that the staff had shown initiative and loyalty to the company. Two got early retirement on the grounds of ill health and the rest took a small reduction in their wages. Over 22 staff, it meant the company saved quite a lot of money.

When you have lost your job through redundancy or downsizing or you bear the burden of having an enormous workload you will know what it is like to be constantly living under a cloud, but remember, clouds can pass just as quickly as they come. No one has the right to make you feel depressed in this way, so start blowing these clouds away little by little and let the light come back into your life again.

Question and answers

Q I am worried that I might be the next to lose my job. A few months ago when we arrived at work we were divided into two groups. I later found out the other group had lost their jobs and had been escorted from the factory. Our group was told that on this occasion we were lucky: we had been the ones to keep our jobs; but things could change if we did not get all the work done. This has put us all under a great deal of pressure, and we all feel unhappy and depressed and scared to do anything about it. I would like to change jobs but have had this one for 15 years since I left school.

A Although they may have had to cut down on the workforce this sounds a very draconian way to go about it. By wielding the big stick they hope to instil fear and keep anyone from complaining. Fear is one of the biggest hurdles people have to overcome. What you have to ask yourself is how long you can go on working in this kind of atmosphere. Maybe it is time to move on. Keep an eye on the job market and wait and see what comes along. Just doing this will make you feel that you are taking charge of your life, and that is a good start.

Q I was one of those who lost my job when the hospital where I worked cut down on the number of staff they employed. Prior to this there had been an investigation into some missing medical supplies. I knew it had nothing to do with me, so although interested in what was going on I was not worried. They never caught the culprit but a month later I was among four people who were made redundant. Their explanation was that they were sending out a lot of the laundry now to contractors. Although I know this to be true I can't help worrying that they may have thought that I had something to do with the missing supplies. This is really making me depressed; they gave me a very good reference but this has not lessened or dispelled this worry.

A You know you had nothing to do with the stolen goods so stop doing this to yourself. They would not have given you a glowing reference if they had suspected you had anything to do with this. Redundancy makes people feel insecure and other worries creep in, but you have every reason to push these away and tell yourself you have nothing to worry about.

4

Team Management and Working to Speed

Team management . . . otherwise known as keeping an eye on your friends and colleagues and trying to keep one step ahead of them!

This has been introduced in many companies under the guise of giving everyone the chance to influence decision-making which in turn will give an uplift to business, commerce and industry. It has, however, proved to be one of the biggest instigators of unhappiness and depression in the workplace. Although it can vary from one company to another, usually the structure changed from having staff who reported to their section leaders, who in turn were responsible to the management, to teams of staff who run themselves and have a manager they are accountable to plus a coach who is there to give them guidance. Teams have regular meetings to discuss how to cope with the work and how they can improve the running of their department.

Nothing wrong with that, you may think, but that's not where it stops. Teams also look at and discuss in front of everyone the performance of individuals – whether they have had too much time off sick, made or received too many personal phone calls, or, in other people's opinion, work too slowly. It can get very personal and threatening to a person's self-esteem at times. This is particularly relevant when bonuses are offered in individual teams. People can get very aggrieved if they feel someone is holding back the chance of all of them getting a bonus.

All the teams report to the manager who is ultimately responsible for the day-to-day running and work of the teams. It would be the manager who would sort out any confrontational problems that the teams can't deal with themselves. The coach has the responsibility of charting different skills within the teams and arranging any training that might be needed.

Although this system has worked well for a lot of people, there are many whose lives have been made a misery because of it. Here are three case histories.

Olive worked for an insurance company who decided to adopt team management. When it first came about everyone was a bit dubious, but gradually they accepted it and Olive was one of the most enthusiastic members of her team.

Her friend Susan, however, who she had worked with for 11 years, hated the whole thing. She was a hard worker and good at her job but just wanted to be left to get on with it without having everybody else chipping in and telling her how she could do the job better. Susan found it very difficult to speak up at the meeting, she preferred to just sit and listen, but Olive was not having that. 'You must have an opinion,' she would bark at Susan. 'Why should the rest of us have to tax our brains while you sit there like a lemon and don't make any input?' Not content to have her say at the meeting, Olive would often badger Susan over lunch or in the car, and even if they met socially. What had been a lovely easygoing friendship changed, and Susan started making excuses so that she didn't have to meet Olive at lunchtimes or socially out of work.

Even when she tried to explain how she felt to Olive, she found her words were falling on deaf ears because that wasn't what Olive, or the others for that matter, wanted to hear.

It is amazing how groups can quickly gang up on one person and Susan found herself as number one on the agenda, with her attitude to work as a team member being the subject for discussion at the next meeting. Needless to say she felt upset, humiliated and depressed about the whole thing. Her input at the meeting was to burst into tears, and the outcome was the others felt they would have to refer her 'problem' to their manager.

Susan's work had never been in question before; she had worked efficiently and quickly, seldom making mistakes. Yes, she had always been quiet but that hadn't been a problem before – perhaps that was why Olive had formed a friendship with her for all these years. Susan was a good listener and Olive needed a sounding board for her opinions; only when they became personal in this way had it caused Susan a problem. At the meeting with the manager she found him more understanding but she came away under no illusions that he too thought she was letting the side down. Susan became more depressed and handed in her notice. Olive still works for the company; she made an initial contact with Susan after she left, saying they must meet up sometime, but neither of them got in contact again.

Susan is now a dental receptionist where there is definitely a team but she is left to organize her own workload.

Terry saw team management as a bit of a laugh until the day they took him to task over his smoking. When the pressures at work had built up, Terry's cigarette consumption had soared from ten a day to nearly thirty. With a no-smoking ban imposed on the whole building, Terry would take himself off up to ten times a day for a quick cigarette. Although he considered it 'quick', his colleagues didn't: at the next team meeting he was told that they had calculated that he was missing from his desk for one hour and 50 minutes each day, and this didn't include his lunch break. They produced a stopwatch and a chart they'd kept to prove it.

'That's over nine hours a week,' they told him, 'Longer than one working day, and that means we're having to do the work that you aren't getting done.'

Obviously it was an unfair situation for his colleagues, but being told this by them *en masse* made his self-confidence wither and his stress levels soar.

Over the coming weeks he tried hard to kick the habit, but even with the help of patches and hypnotherapy he wasn't successful. He didn't even like to go to the toilet any more for fear that the others would think he had gone for a crafty cigarette. Eventually he managed to get through the day with just a couple of cigarettes at lunch-time, but he never trusted anyone after that and dreaded team management meetings in case anyone else had it in for him again.

Our third case history is about Sarah and Kelly, who started the same week and had been working together for three years. When team management was introduced where they worked, they were told that everything was to be totally open and that from now on teams would not only assess each other's potential and faults but also whether they should get a pay rise or note. For reasons Kelly and Sarah could never understand, their colleagues decided that they didn't deserve a pay rise that year or a bonus. Words such as productivity, working to speed and skills matrix (which I shall cover later) were bandied about, and two pretty confident 18-year-olds went home with their confidence in shreds. Sarah's mum had died only three months previously; just as she was coming to terms with it, this happened and it made her depressed for several months. Meanwhile Kelly tried hard to apply herself to the job and was getting encouragement, duly deserved, from the rest of the team. Sarah saw this as Kelly trying to get one over on her and make her look like the office idiot. Coupled with her bereavement Sarah became very depressed, had four months off work and never returned to this job. Kelly stayed on at the job and they are still friends.

Like many others who have always coped and got on well with their work, Susan, Terry and Sarah felt they were being made into victims by team management. They felt the idea behind it was sound but that it gave people a sense of power that they could wield quite cruelly, and that in their cases it had led to them becoming depressed and to two of them looking for work elsewhere.

If you feel this is happening to you, don't feel there are no avenues open to you. If your work is in question ask to see the coach and discuss this. Before you go make a list of the things you want to discuss and make the list concise. This will make the interview easier for you because you will be taking some control over what is to be discussed and you won't be floundering around from one grievance to another.

Ask the coach for help and training in any areas that you are being questioned on by the others or that bother you. It is also a good idea for a week before the interview to keep a diary of the work that you do each day and the time you spend. If the speed of your work is in question this will help you to clarify whether you are wasting time or achieving all you can. The important thing that all team members should remember is that not everyone can work at the same speed: some work quickly but may make mistakes, others work slower, more methodically and seldom make mistakes. Quality and quantity should never be confused.

If you feel the coach hasn't been able to reassure you ask for another meeting, this time with the manager.

When it's a more personal matter such as Susan's quietness and inability to contribute at meetings, it is the manager that you need to speak to. Unfortunately in Susan's case her manager opted for a cop-out by telling her that teams were here to stay and she would have to make more effort. He didn't try to help build her confidence or speak to other members of the team, which he should have. In many of the letters I receive, a meeting with the manager has helped everyone involved to realize its members are still human and all different, unlike computers which play such a big part in all areas of the workplace today.

Team management gives a lot of power to people who often don't know how to use it; you may have heard the saying 'power went to his head', and in this case it is often true. Another saying is 'the weakest went to the wall', and this accounts for many people becoming depressed because of the pressures team management can bring. Those with the strongest characters rise to the challenge, but others often lose confidence very quickly and this affects their ability to work as well as their state of mind.

If all else fails, speak to Personnel (Human Resources). Maybe a fresh start with a new team might be the answer.

Working to speed means workers are under pressure to work harder and produce more work in the same or less time, often in competition with colleagues. This has caused a lot of distress and depression across the whole of the work industry.

Goals are constantly being moved in an endeavour to get workers to produce more work. This happened to Colin, Gillian and Pete.

Colin worked on an assembly line in a factory, Gillian as a packer for a cosmetics firm and Pete's job is with a large well-known supermarket group.

Productivity bonuses on a yearly basis were brought in at the factory where Colin worked. Workers were told to increase their output to a a certain level over a period of a month, which they did. Two months later their boss told them they had done well but he thought that they could do even better, so targets were raised, only for the same thing to happen several times over the coming months. It got to the point where Colin and the others dreaded going to work because the targets were now unobtainable and so were the bonuses. Colin became depressed because he lives in an area with high unemployment and knew that there would be others who would jump at his job if he couldn't cope. He was scared to take the antidepressants the doctor offered in case they slowed him down even further. He wasn't alone: all his colleagues were under stress, some depressed like him and others having minor accidents because of rushing and not taking enough care.

In circumstances like this it is important to present a united front to the management and say that the goals are unrealistic and unfair and that safety is being jeopardized. Where safety is an issue you can also take the matter up with he Health and Safety Executive and get advice.

In Gillian's case it was very similar except that she had a history of depression, which was made worse by the introduction of working to speed. Having given up her job as a supervisor for the company following a bout of depression, she had felt the packing job suited her because it didn't put her under a lot of pressure and she felt she had made a good recovery. A year later, when new measures to increase output came into practice, Gillian found the packaging piling up and herself at the receiving end of rebukes from her manager. Often she would stay late to try and clear the backlog, but this put her under even more pressure as she had a family to get back to and her husband got irritated when she wasn't there when he got in from work.

When she wrote to me she was off with depression and felt all the confidence and progress she had built up prior to this had now gone for good.

I met Pete when he came to me for counselling. He was off work with depression having been given a change of job, which involved meeting the lorries as they came into the delivery bays in the early hours of morning so that stocks were put in place before the store opened.

Having always had a day job he found it difficult to change his sleep pattern to fit in with going to bed at 7 p.m. and getting up at 1 a.m.

He had also been put under a lot of pressure to do more work. To begin with he would only have to supervise the unloading of one or two large lorries, but by the end of three months it was often three or four. He was paid to work until 7.45 each morning, but often the lorries were still being unloaded as the supermarket opened. He was told by his supervisor that he wasn't working fast enough or making others do the same. Although he tried to tell them there was more work to do in the same amount of time they wouldn't listen and told him goals had to be reached, time was money and if he couldn't stand the pace there were others who could.

When I counselled him he was off work with depression. He was being constantly asked by the company when he was coming back and was scared he would lose his job altogether. With a wife and three children to support, life was far from easy. Eventually he returned to work but was still on antidepressants and was scared he wouldn't be able to work at the speed that they expected.

If you feel you are the victim of working to speed and have become depressed because of it, it is very important that you tell your employer as soon as you can and ask for help. Put the ball firmly in their court; if your immediate supervisor or manager refuses to listen, go higher. You really have nothing to lose. Often fear of the unknown will stop people taking matters into their own hands; they are scared that they will lose their job or be labelled a troublemaker.

What you have to remember is that your immediate supervisor or manager is under pressure from the top and is passing the burden down to you. Perhaps they are equally dissatisfied with the way things are. If they are seen to be lenient with you it reflects on them, which is why you have to be firm and take control. Put your concerns in writing and take them along to any meetings that you can arrange. Make sure you couple this with a list of suggestions which you feel would improve things as well as taking some of the pressures off yourself. At the end of the meeting leave copies with the manager for them to read after you have gone. Management hate what they see as whingers and those who rock the boat, but if you can approach them in a positive way they are more likely to take on board what you have to say.

Finally a word about skills matrix, which is a scheme to help individuals reach their full potential by having a scale of skills that they can work to. Employees are encouraged to learn new skills and gradually move up the scale as their knowledge increases. Some companies pay individual bonuses for this, while others will evaluate a whole team's progress up the learning scale. For instance, some shops will offer individual one-off cash sums to sales staff when they become knowledgeable on a certain aspect of the work they do – in a DIY store sales staff may get bonuses each time they can reach a certain standard in electrical, plumbing, decorating, gardening and timber areas of the company.

Another company may send their staff on Outward Bound courses to see how they perform as a team and who shows outstanding characteristics that might make them management material at a later date. Although some people find both of these aspects daunting, fewer people become depressed over skills matrix than the other issues that we have covered.

Sometimes you need to stand up for yourself, and if you manage to do this you will be surprised how easy it becomes after the first time.

Questions and answers

Q I am a single mum with a child at nursery school. I work for a health trust as a receptionist three days a week and a medical records clerk for two days, both from 8.30 a.m. to 3 p.m. Over the past year we have been put into teams and once a week we have to meet together to report on our job. This is not a problem for me except that they always arrange these meetings at the end of the day, around 4 o'clock, which means that once a week I have to pay a childminder two hours extra when I'm not getting paid for this time. The others say it breaks up the day to have it at any other time. I am beginning to feel very depressed every Thursday when these meetings take place and can't concentrate because I am constantly watching the clock. What can I do about this? Everyone else works until 5 p.m., then the meeting ends and you can't see them for dust.

A You are paid to work until 3 o'clock and you shouldn't be expected to hang around for an hour for the meeting to start and spend another hour at the meeting when the rest of the staff are being paid to attend. Tell your line manager that you need to be paid for your time and extra childminding. The alternative is that you won't be able to go unless you bring your toddler with you. I doubt if they will relish the thought of having a tired irritable toddler at the meeting each week, and if they want you there, they will sort something out.

Q I am worried about my 24-year-old daughter who is off work with depression. She was made to feel useless by the people she thought were her friends at work. She is dyslexic but refused to tell her employer because she thought it would go against her getting the job. Now there is much more pressure to reach targets and her dyslexia is showing both in her written and phone work. She found that she was constantly got at because of the mistakes she was making yet she still refused to tell them about her problem. Should I phone and tell her employer in the hope they will understand?

A Not a good idea for you to get involved, but if you can encourage her to tell them herself I think this would be a good idea. They can't be expected to understand if she is not completely honest with them. Once she does this I think the worry and depression will start to lift and she will be able to go back to work, and hopefully they will be much more understanding.

5

Men, Women and Depression

In this chapter we look at the similarities and differences that cause depression for men and women and how each cope. It's a sad fact that men see depression as weakness and often won't admit that they are depressed.

Although it is likely that men suffer with depression just as much as women, statistics show that they find it much harder to seek help or talk to friends or relatives about it, than women do. Perhaps this is because women have probably had more contact over the years with their doctor. They may go regularly for contraception, smear tests, during and after pregnancy and with their children's ailments and health care, which can mean they have a good rapport with their doctor. They know their doctor is more likely to see their depression as an illness rather than a weakness because they have seen them at other times when they have been well and able to cope.

Men on the other hand visit their GPs much less, some rarely, and haven't built up any kind of relationship with their doctor. This means at a time when they are feeling at an all-time low and guilty for not being able to cope, they are faced with someone they hardly know to discuss what they see as a weakness.

Perhaps the past and how men have been viewed has a lot to answer for. Men have until recently, when women have changed the scenario, been the carers, the providers and the protectors. With the advent of much stronger women wanting to assert themselves both at home and in the workplace this role has been eroded, leaving the men confused and uncertain about their role.

Strengths, power, success and being able to achieve have always been associated with men. Right from when they were little most men were told by their mothers 'boys don't cry' and were brought up with these great expectations of themselves, like a yoke around their necks. No wonder they get scared when they become depressed: as their strength, self-confidence and will to achieve slips away, the guilt builds up only to compound the depression.

Women on the other hand don't see tears or feeling stress as a weakness. They have always been known as the gentler sex, which in turn spells fragile and vulnerable. Although most would not describe themselves as this today, women do have more of an ability than men to accept that depression is an illness and that it is nothing to feel ashamed of, whereas men do feel ashamed. To admit that you are fragile, vulnerable and need help is not an easy option for a man. It strikes at the heart of his self-esteem, especially when his ability to work and provide for his family is affected. To admit that he needs help and that he needs to rely on others doesn't come easily, even if it is only for a short while.

Here are the case histories of two people, a man and his wife, that illustrate the differences in the way they viewed depression, how they dealt with it and how it affected each other's lives. It illustrates different attitudes men and women often have.

Gary and Diana had been married for 16 years when Diana became depressed after the death of her sister in a road accident. Although Gary loved her he had no patience with people who suffered 'things of the mind', as he put it. He had been brought up in a rough area where men had to be tough to survive. He got very irritated with Diana at times, and if it hadn't been for the support of her friends and an understanding GP her depression would have lasted much longer.

Shortly after her sister died Diana realized she was becoming depressed. To begin with there had been an overwhelming sadness, following by anger and then despair. She found doing things that had always been a pleasure didn't interest her any more, and the more mundane things such as shopping, housework and even getting up in the morning too much of an effort.

Fortunately she talked to friends and her mother and went to see her GP, who put here on a course of antidepressants, but it took over a year for Diana to get her life back on track again. During this time Gary, who was a market stallholder, realized she was ill and towards the end of her illness stopped getting annoyed when she wouldn't go and help him on the stall.

About two years later Gary got into a fight with one of the other market traders who had set up a stall very close to his own selling the same goods. He had complained to the market manager, who said it was fair competition and that he had been lucky to have cornered that end of the market for so long. The effect on his trade was minimal as people tended to drift to the other stall for a few weeks and then come back to him. But emotionally he couldn't let it drop; he saw it as the worst thing that could have happened to him and no amount of reassurance from Diana, who was now back working full-time on the stall, did any good.

Eaten up with anger which spilled over into all areas of his life, he became irritable, short-tempered and unwell. He couldn't concentrate, he got headaches, felt sick and had difficulty making even the simplest of decisions. Diana knew deep down he was depressed, but when she suggested this to him he got into a rage and told her that she was the weak one, not him.

Over the next six months he got worse. He wasn't interested in eating, his attitude to everything and everyone was negative, and he went from being one of the most popular people in the market with the stallholders to one they avoided. Regular customers noticed a difference in him, and Diana dreaded when anyone commented directly to either of them about the changes in him because he got into such a state. No longer did he get angry: instead he would try avoiding customers and sat for long periods in the van, saying he got tired.

On one occasion he did go to see his doctor because he needed a tetanus jab, but when the doctor asked him how he was he told him he had headaches but nothing else. The doctor gave him a prescription and suggested he get his eyes tested and then come back the following week for a complete check-up. Gary didn't go.

Eighteen months after the fight Gary's depression was getting worse. He now had difficulty getting up each day; he said there was no point as he wasn't making a living out of the stall any more. Diana, who did all the books, knew this was untrue and tried to reassure him, but he wouldn't listen. By now Gary was also drinking far too heavily, and more often than not Diana would have to run the stall alone, which meant going to the Cash and Carry and setting up the stall each day on her own.

Gary still refused to accept that he was depressed and Diana, understanding from own experience of depression, tried to help him in every way that she could. Eventually she went to her GP who agreed to come out and see Gary. It was obvious that Gary was very depressed and he cried like a baby all the time the doctor was there. The doctor wanted Gary to go into hospital but he refused, saying he wasn't depressed and he wasn't weak. Eventually it was agreed that the doctor would visit him once a week until he was well enough to come to the surgery. Diana got him to take the antidepressants and he seemed after a month to be making some progress. Then one day Diana came home from the stall to find that he had committed suicide.

She came to me for counselling shortly after his death and said he had been so ashamed at being depressed. He thought the people at the market would be laughing behind his back and that he would never be able to face them again.

Gary's abhorrence of any kind of mental illness and seeing it as a weakness in sufferers stopped him from getting help earlier. Diana still blames herself for not being there that day and thinks if she had gone to the doctor's on his behalf earlier he might still be alive.

The truth is that unlike Diana, who didn't feel ashamed of being depressed, Gary refused to admit that he was suffering with depression right up until the day he died, because he saw it as a weakness and this was something he could never admit to. Diana gave up the stall and took a job in a supermarket instead.

Depression can affect the sexuality of both men and women. When you are depressed you feel tired, unmotivated and less good about your body. For women this means feeling less sexy than they used to and probably too tired and uninterested to be bothered. The one thing they often do feel, though, is guilt that they are depriving their partners, and they live in constant dread of bedtime and maybe having to 'perform' when they don't want to.

For men it can affect them in several ways. Some lose confidence altogether and become impotent; this means they have difficulty in getting or maintaining an erection. It is important to mention at this point that it can happen the other way around and that impotence can actually be the cause of depression. If this is the case, discussing it with your GP may be embarrassing but it could help both your sexual problem and your depression. Some men have intercourse regularly during their period of depression but don't find it as satisfying as it used to be, while others try to have more sex than they used to in an attempt to restore their self-esteem and make themselves feel better. It is important to remember that some antidepressants can reduce sex drive in both men and women. If this happens it will make things much easier if you go to the doctor with your partner and discuss this, so that your partner understands that this is part of the illness and not a rejection of them. The good news is that as your depression improves so will your sex drive.

With more and more women returning to work after having a baby rather than staying at home to look after them, it is inevitable that some will become depressed. Not only are they juggling a full-time job at work and another one at home, they now have the added responsibility of a baby. It is bad enough having sleepless nights when you are going to be at home during the day, but to have to get up and go and do a responsible full-time job is often far too much. Many women suffer with post-natal depression, and taking on such a heavy workload just aggravates the situation. Whether you work for financial reasons or for your own sake, sometimes considering part-time or job share is a far better option than returning to work full-time and putting yourself under so much pressure.

Many women go back for financial reasons, but an increasing number do so because they don't want to lose their status or the position they have reached at work. If they stay out of their workplace for a few years to bring up the children, they fear that they will no longer be employable at the same level or that jobs may not be available.

Although it is a well-known fact that mothers can become depressed after childbirth, it is only more recently that research has shown that about one in ten fathers also suffer psychological problems at this time. This shouldn't come as too much of a surprise to us, as it well known that major events in our lives – even good ones such as moving house – can bring on a period of depression.

A baby in the family affects a man's life very much: suddenly he has new responsibilities that can cause anxieties. Sleepless nights affect him, too, and it can make it difficult for him to concentrate at work.

Feelings of being rejected are not uncommon either. A baby seems to take up so much of a woman's time that there seems to be none left for the man in her life. Many men feel they are pushed to the back of the queue and have to take second place to their children in their partner's affections. Many women also lose interest in sex, which again makes them feel rejected. This is sad when the main reason for this is plain and simple ... tiredness!

Post-natal depression is very common during the weeks and months following a birth but very few people stop and consider that a man can become depressed as well. Fathers are more likely to become depressed if their partner is suffering with post-natal depression or if they are not getting on. Either way, counselling might help both to cope with and overcome the stresses and problems of being parents.

All these factors can cause depression, especially if an employer doesn't understand when the man needs more time off or is tired and finding it more difficult to cope at work.

As I mentioned earlier in this chapter, men tend to see themselves as the providers and so when unemployment strikes it is a traumatic shock. Research has shown that up to one in seven men who become unemployed will develop a depressive illness if they are out of work for some months. Women are also affected badly by unemployment, but are far more likely than the men to be optimistic and take whatever work they can to tide them over until the right thing comes along. Although some do become depressed it is not such a high percentage as it is for men.

Women are far more likely to put their unemployment down to bad luck and being in the wrong place at the wrong time than men, who see it as personal failure and are riddled with feelings of guilt and shame. For some unknown reason we are brought up to feel that when things go wrong it must be our fault and that we have to feel guilty about it. This is total nonsense, because most of the things that happen in our lives are due to circumstances and not because we make them happen.

When a woman is depressed she is more likely to say to her GP that she is feeling weepy, sad, miserable or depressed, whereas men are more likely to talk about physical symptoms than psychological or emotional ones. This may be a very important reason why some doctors don't diagnose depression in men. So it is important that they tell their doctors exactly how they are feeling rather than holding back and not getting the help that they need. Although women may also feel ashamed that they are depressed and that they are not coping very well, most of them will have known someone who has suffered in this way before and won't feel they are alone. Many will want to talk about what is happening to them and gain comfort from listening to other people's experiences. Men on the other hand may see it as being weak and unmanly and won't even tell those close to them how wretched they feel.

Retirement can also bring about depression for some men and women. This is particularly so for single men and women with very little else in their lives other than their jobs. They may become depressed in the months or even the years preceding their retirement, with men and women experiencing similar fears and worries.

Usually when they do retire they find all kinds of things to do and realize that there is a whole new world out there waiting to be explored and that life doesn't have to revolve around work, and the depression soon lifts.

In the workplace women and men can be equally affected by restructuring, changes in contracts and working conditions. It's fair to say that men might be the last to admit it but they feel the strain just as much as their female counterparts. Perhaps if they talked more about their worries rather than just putting up with things they would get over their depression far more quickly than most of them do. They also have to shed the misconception that depression is a sign of weakness and unmanly. Both men and women who are depressed ask me, 'Will I every be normal again?' The answer is, 'Yes' provided you recognize what is happening and get the help that you need. The depression won't last for ever, and once you have recovered you should regain your confidence and energy and start to enjoy your life again.

Questions and answers

Q I work with a girl who is either off sick with depression or at work whinging that she can't cope. Our boss suffered with depression after his wife died and he says I should be more understanding. The trouble is, Vicky, she isn't doing her fair share of work and it all falls on me. The work has to be done and she is getting paid for doing virtually nothing. It really gets on my nerves. Why should the rest of us have to put up with these inadequate women like her when we men have to cope? On top of this she is the queen of sarcasm.

A Depression is a much misunderstood illness, and if you have not suffered with it yourself then it will be hard to appreciate how debilitating it is. Your colleague is lucky to have such an understanding boss, but I think he needs also to take into account the pressure her illness is putting on you. Of course it is right that he should be supportive of her, but it isn't fair to expect you to take on the work of two people. He has to realize that this is putting a strain on you and could make you ill as well. He sounds the sort of person that you could talk to, but don't be aggressive or come on too strong or you will get nowhere. Start by asking if you can discuss something that is worrying you and tell him that you are finding it hard to do her work as well as your own. Unless you tell him he won't know how you feel and he may not realize the unfairness of the situation. As for her sarcastic behaviour, most people who are sarcastic think they are being clever and witty. They are the first to say they don't suffer fools gladly, but in most cases it is their own insecurities that cause them to put others down to make themselves seem more interesting or well informed. In your colleague's case it may be the way that she builds a shell around herself so that she doesn't get hurt.

Q I am really worried about my husband. He used to be such a jolly man, yet over the past few months he has become withdrawn and depressed but will not see his doctor. He set up a business with a man who he had worked with for many years. My husband held one third of the business and did all the repairs and rebuilding of second-hand computers, while the other man had to put in two-thirds of the money to start with and ran the sales side. Over the past four years the business has grown and we were starting to reap the financial benefits. I suppose we should have read the warning signs earlier that things were going to change when his partner informed him that his son was training to be a computer maintenance and service engineer. Four months ago his partner told my husband, who is in his fifties, that his son would be joining the company and he wanted my husband to show him the ropes. Now my husband finds responsible tasks have been taken away from him and given to the son, which is making him feel insecure. About a month ago his partner asked him if he had thought about retiring and my husband knew then that they wanted him out. Next day his partner said he wanted to buy my husband's shares in the business for his son. My husband refused, and now they are hardly speaking to him and he is so depressed. What can I do? It has made me depressed as well. Today I have had to go to the doctor's and have been put on antidepressants, yet my husband refuses to admit he is depressed and won't get help.

A This is not an uncommon situation – partnerships that start out fine often reach this kind of watershed. Your husband shouldn't make any major decisions while he feels depressed. Instead he should get help from his doctor and see his solicitor to find out what his rights are. It sounds a pretty miserable atmosphere to be working in, and he may well decide at the end of the day that the best thing to do would be to sell his part of the business and make a fresh start. But it needs a lot of thought, and he has to look after himself and his health first and foremost. It is sad that this has made you depressed as well.

6

The Importance of Getting Help

One of the first people I ever counselled was a very nice young man called Owen when I started work in a GP practice in south London. Owen was in his thirties and a high flyer with one of the big banks in the City of London; he worked as a trouble-shooter and was sent all over the world to sort out problems that arose in foreign branches.

The envy of most of his friends, he was nice-looking, intelligent, comfortably off and confident. That was until the day the bank insisted that he took a holiday, something he hadn't done for six years. 'Everyone needs a break,' his manager told him, 'and you have been working non-stop for too long.' Reluctantly he agreed to take four weeks' holiday. Little did he know that it would be 17 months before he would be able to go back to work again.

When Owen came to me for counselling I knew from his doctor that once he had stopped work he hadn't been able to switch off or relax. Instead he had become tense, and by the second week he was suffering with upset stomach, headaches, tiredness and aching limbs. He thought he had flu and phoned in sick, something he had never done before. After a few days he expected the symptoms to ease, but they didn't and he started feeling sick, anxious and lifeless. Over the next few weeks he visited his doctor regularly because he needed to be signed off sick from work. Each time he presented physical symptoms to his GP but never mentioned the fact that he was feeling increasingly anxious and depressed. Even when his doctor asked him outright if he was feeling low or depressed or whether anything was worrying him he would refuse to admit it, even to himself.

He had no end of tests done to eliminate all kinds of physical illnesses and dismissed having counselling out of hand.

Then one day he said he was going to return to work, as he blamed being at home for making him feel so ill. He never made it: instead he painted the inside of all the windows in his house with black paint and took to his bed. That is where his mother found him days later, dirty, unkempt and having eaten virtually nothing. The room smelt dreadful as he hadn't even bothered to get up to go to the toilet.

His doctor admitted him to a psychiatric hospital that day and he stayed there for six weeks. When discharged it was agreed that he would visit his GP once a week and also come to me for counselling.

I saw Owen on a weekly basis for nearly a year, at the end of which he returned to work. For Owen, stopping work, taking away the structure of his day and being unable to relax had triggered his depression. He had been in the fast lane for so long that he went to pieces when he wasn't. He was so used to being in charge and the one who sorted out problems that it came as a shock to find that he was having problems himself. For nearly six months he had been too scared to tell his doctor the real reasons why he needed help. He had never had much time for people who suffered with depression and in the past had often described them as malingerers. How could he admit to himself, let alone to anyone else, how he felt? His physical symptoms were all genuine and part and parcel of being depressed, but had Owen been able to say he was feeling down, sad, miserable or depressed his doctor would have been able to diagnose depression and start treating him sooner, and Owen wouldn't have suffered so much.

This is quite a common problem. A lot of people will see their GP and present physical symptoms, all genuine, but omit to say they are feeling depressed. Some will spend their visit to their doctor describing their physical symptoms, then just as they are about to go out of the door they will say something like, 'By the way, doctor, I have been feeling a bit miserable lately.' It's called the 'hand on the door' syndrome, and is very common – often the time when the GP first learns of the real reason for their visit.

In the majority of cases depression comes on very gradually, and it is not always easy to recognize if this is happening to you. It can also affect people in varying degrees, from a sense of sadness to deep depression. However it affects you, it is important to see your doctor as quickly as possible. Early diagnosis and treatment will lead to an early recovery. Honesty about your symptoms plays a crucial role as well. Don't be ashamed or afraid to say you are feeling sad, miserable or depressed. Presenting safe symptoms in the hope that the doctor might just be able to make you better is simply putting things off and letting them get worse. Mental illness is nothing to be ashamed of.

If you had a broken leg, stomach pains, headaches or any other physical symptoms you wouldn't think it shameful to have to go to the doctor for help. Well, depression is no different. It is an illness just like any other.

If you are nervous about seeing your doctor at the best of times then having to go with depression isn't going to be easy, especially if you are feeling confused and having difficulty concentrating.

The following doctor's checklist is designed to help you cope with your visit and come away with your questions answered and logged so that you can read it when you get home. You will need to fill in Part A of the checklist before you go to the surgery. Part B, which I have made as short as I can, needs to be filled in while you are with your doctor. If you feel too confused to do this ask your doctor to do it for you. He won't mind because it is better that you understand what is going on rather than get home and be worried.

So here is the checklist:

Checklist

PART A (give to your doctor when you visit)

Symptoms (tick how you are feeling)

- feeling down;
- agitated;
- lack of concentration;
- tired all the time;
- anxious;
- sleep problems;
- (add your own symptoms including physical ones to those that you have ticked).

I have felt like this for   years/months/weeks

Other things I would like to ask or tell my doctor

PART B

Doctor's diagnosis

Medication prescribed

Medication to be taken

Is there anything I should not do when taking this medication?

Next visit

Advice from doctor

By doing this you not only come away with the information you might have otherwise forgotten but you are also making a shared contract with your GP. Remember, this is your body and it is up to you to decide, with the expertise of your doctor, what will help you to get better. If you are worried about taking antidepressants tell your doctor and ask for an explanation of how they work and if there will be any side-effects.

Ask your doctor how long it will be before the tablets start to work and how you are likely to feel until they start to have an effect. If you feel this is all too much to cope with, ask a friend or family member to go with you. It is very important that you are in control and instigate this shared contract (decision) on what your treatment should be with your GP rather than just accepting whatever you are offered. No one should go to their GP and come out clutching a prescription with no idea what is happening to them. Today most GPs are very knowledgeable on depression, the medication and other ways of helping sufferers. It is in their interest as well as yours to make shared decisions rather than have a patient who is unsure about their treatment, stops taking medication because they haven't given it long enough to work, and is unwell for longer because of this.

It may seem early in this book to be talking about the effect depression may be having on your sex life but I make no excuse for this. Some of you may not be having problems but there will be an awful lot of you who are, and this is something else which you might like to discuss with your doctor.

Feelings of sadness, hopelessness and helplessness are typical features of depression. Coupled with the tiredness that depressed people feel, loss of sex drive is very common. If you are depressed and have lost interest in sex, don't worry – you are not alone. Surveys show that two out of three people lose interest in sex when they are depressed, and this lack of interest is a symptom of depression probably caused by an imbalance in the brain chemistry.

Among the most common sexual problems encountered are

- lack of interest due to tiredness and sad feelings;
- not being able to get sexually aroused;
- not being able to get or maintain an erection;
- premature ejaculation;
- not being able to ejaculate or have an orgasm.

Problems are often made worse by partners who don't understand. If this is the case try to get your partner to go with you to see the doctor, so that they can be reassured that this is all part of the illness and that as your depression lifts your sex drive will return. Relate are also a good source of help when you are experiencing problems of this kind.

Although today's antidepressants are very effective in treating depression, some antidepressants may make sexual problems worse or give new ones. If this happens don't stop taking it. Discuss the problems with your doctor, who may change or alter the dose of your medication.

Some doctors may ask about your sex life, while others may say nothing because they are worried that they may offend you. If you are worried about how to broach the subject, try saying, 'I seem to have lost interest in sex, is this normal?' or, 'Since I have been on antidepressants it seems to have affected my sex life.' This will open up the conversation and enable you to get the help you need.

If you fill in the relevant section of the following questionnaire (Figure 4 for women, Figure 5 for men), this might help you understand and discuss the problems you are having with your doctor.

Figure 4

Questionnaire for women

Tick one box for each question

How have your sexual feelings changed?

Totally disappeared	☐
Reduced a little	☐
Reduced a lot	☐
Increased	☐

Do you get aroused like you used to?

No, not at all	☐
Not as much as I used to	☐
Same as usual	☐
More than usual	☐

Do you enjoy sex at the moment?

No, not at all	☐
Less than I used to	☐
Same as usual	☐
More than usual	☐

Has your ability to reach orgasm changed?

Yes	☐
No	☐

How would you describe your orgasms now?

Better	☐
Worse	☐
Same	☐

Figure 5

Questionnaire for men

Tick one box for each question

Has your desire to have sex changed?

Totally disappeared	☐
Reduced	☐
Same	☐
Increased	☐

Can you enjoy sex at the moment?

No, not at all	☐
Less than usual	☐
Same as usual	☐
Better than usual	☐

Can you get your normal erection?

Never	☐
Sometimes	☐
Usually	☐
Always	☐

Can you maintain your normal erection?

Yes, as usual	☐
Yes, but not for as long as usual	☐
Hardly at all	☐
Never	☐

Do you have difficulty in ejaculating (coming)?

Always	☐
Usually	☐
Sometimes	☐
Never	☐

If you repeat this questionnaire from time to time it will help you and your doctor monitor your progress.

I have talked about a shared contract (decision between you and your GP) and I can't emphasize enough the importance of staying in control. This applies right through your illness: from the day when you first see your doctor, make sure that your progress and medication are monitored regularly. See the doctor, nurse or the community psychiatric nurse at set intervals. If you feel you are not making progress don't feel afraid to say so. There are many different therapies and medications that your doctor can suggest you try, so keep in control of your treatment as well as your progress. Being in control also applies to your life, relationships and work.

So many people who are depressed try to keep it from their family and friends. Why? Because they are worrying that they are letting down those that they care about. They forget all the things they have done for others in the past, the support they have given when other people have been ill or in trouble. Talk to those close to you, surround yourself with as many loving people as you can. Don't isolate yourself by pushing people who want to help away because you think they will feel sorry for you. Maybe this gives them the chance to show they care. Other people need to be needed as well.

When asking for help the question of whether or not to tell employers and colleagues arises. Depression affects one in four employees each year, so the chances are someone else who works with you will either be feeling depressed as well or has been in the past.

Depression accounts for nearly 20 per cent of all sickness absences in the workplace, and if you think about it carefully you will be able to identify others who may be suffering just as you are. Friends and colleagues may have noticed changes in you anyway – perhaps you have become much quieter, tearful sometimes, or your concentration and memory seem to be affected. If someone asks if anything is wrong and you feel you can trust them, tell them you are feeling depressed, rather than getting irritated and fobbing them off. People who bottle things up and try to keep going as if nothing is happening are often the ones who end up having to take time off, whereas those who say how they feel early on are less likely to. Most people know who they can trust, and having just one person who will understand at work will reduce those dreadful feelings of isolation that depression brings.

There will be some who will feel threatened if they find out you are depressed, but remember, the people who feel threatened are usually pretty inadequate themselves or have skeletons in their own cupboards. Your illness may invoke memories of past periods of depression that they may have suffered or the pain that they'd felt when seeing someone they loved who was depressed. Some may see it as a weakness, but that's their problem, not yours. Others may be convinced that you may not be able to do your work and it might all fall on them. It's up to you to put the record straight on this and tell them that if this happens you will be the first to be worried about it and would ask the manager for advice. People get scared of what might happen. If you are honest and try to see things from their point of view as well as your own, they will probably be the ones who turn up trumps and defend you.

Whether or not to tell your employer is another matter. Ask yourself whether you would go to your employer and tell them you were suffering with other ailments unless you needed time off. The answer is probably no; the only difference is if your depression is affecting your work or if the work is affecting your health. Then it is a case of assessing who would be the most understanding person to speak to. If there is a counselling or welfare service available at your company, take advantage of this. The same applies if the company you work for has a nurse or a doctor. Knowing there is a professional who you can turn to at work could make all the difference. Everyone needs help at some time in their life but often they find it hard to ask for it, maybe because they are too proud or scared to be seen as vulnerable. Being depressed adds even more fuel to these insecure feelings and many people wait far too long before seeking the help they need.

Take Marilyn, for instance. She had been struggling for months with a job that had changed so much she hardly recognized it. She also had a husband who was having an affair. It was six months before her best friend at work finally got her to see her doctor. The next couple of months were very difficult for her but gradually she took charge of her life again. She gave her husband an ultimatum and he chose to leave and go and live with the other woman. This set Marilyn back for a while, but gradually she felt better and was able to speak to her manager about the work she was unhappy doing. He arranged for her to be transferred to another department where she did a job which was very similar to the one she used to do. She was glad about this and, unbeknown to her at the time, it suited her manager as he had been debating for a long while her ability to do the job and wanted to replace her. Marilyn got her life back because she finally realized she couldn't do so without help.

The day you wake up with that sinking feeling in the pit of your stomach and dread what lies ahead is the day you need to ask for help, so please make sure you get it. If you do you can be sure you are well on the road to recovery.

Questions and answers

Q My husband has been suffering with depression and is on antidepressants following redundancy. To begin with our sex life was much the same as usual but now it is non-existent. More often than not he is in bed asleep before I get there. If I suggest I have an early night as well he will get agitated and say he can't get to sleep unless he goes up to bed on his own. Sometimes he is awake really early in the morning, but if I try to initiate sex he will roll over with his back towards me and tell me to leave him alone. I know he is ill, but surely it's at times like this that being close really counts?
A Kisses and cuddles maybe, but for many men who are depressed sex isn't an option, either because they feel too low and tired to be bothered or because they physically can't. That medication your husband is taking may be causing him to be temporarily impotent. In other words, he may not be able to get an erection. This on top of being made redundant would be striking right at the heart of his self-esteem. Let him know that you love him, and that there is no pressure on him to do anything sexually but just a cuddle would be lovely in the meantime.

Q I went to see my doctor because I was depressed and he made me feel worse by writing out a prescription as I was trying to explain to him how I was feeling. Then he stood up and packed his things away in his bag and made me feel such a nuisance. I was only in his surgery for a few minutes and it had taken me weeks to pluck up the courage to go. The receptionist knew I was upset when I came out and said he had come in late that morning and was trying to catch up.

A I am sorry that you were treated with such lack of consideration. Fortunately this kind of treatment is not typical of what most doctors offer today. Obviously there is only a short appointment time, but most GPs would suggest another visit if they feel there hasn't been enough time to discuss things in detail. I would suggest you pick another doctor within the group or change doctors, then make an appointment to see them. Hopefully next time you won't be dismissed in such a dreadful way and will get the help that you need.

Q I know my employer's wife has suffered with depression for years because he has often mentioned it. I now find I am feeling depressed, mainly because I am worried that at 55 I could be the next one to be made redundant. This is affecting my work. Should I speak to my employer and tell him the worry is making me depressed? Surely he will understand.

A I think he would understand how you are feeling and he may be able to reassure you that your fears are groundless. That's a chance you will have to take because he may not be able to promise that you will always have a job. But being uncertain is often worse than knowing the truth and causes depression. Perhaps if you knew where you stood it would be far better.

7

Will I Become an Addict If I Take Antidepressants?

'Will I become dependent on them if I take antidepressants?' is the question most frequently asked by those who turn to their doctors for help. The short answer is no, antidepressants are not addictive. This is a common misapprehension. People tend to confuse antidepressants with a type of tranquillizer called benzodiazepines. Tranquillizers are habit-forming and people do find it difficult to stop taking them. Fortunately that is not the case with antidepressants and they are quite safe to take for long periods of time.

However, all medicines can have side-effects, even ones you can buy at the chemist or drugstore without prescriptions. So it is important to weigh up any unpleasant side-effects against the distress which is caused by depression. Even if you do get side-effects you will normally only get them for a limited period of time whereas your depression, if left untreated, could last for months or even years.

Different antidepressants have different side-effects, so if you find one does not suit you, go back to your GP and ask to try another. You may find you have to try several until you find the one that suits you.

Antidepressants take about two to three weeks to 'kick in' before you start to feel any better. Some people say they felt worse during this period of time than they did before they started taking the medication. For some people it can take a month, and in elderly people as long as six to eight weeks. The reason for this is that antidepressants need to reach a certain level before they begin to work. The level of the dose varies for different antidepressants and different people, and for some you need to start low and build up to the effective dose.

Sadly, lots of people stop too soon – they do not think the drug is working because no one has explained this to them or how long they need to take it for. It is very important to persevere and give the treatment its full chance to work. During this time, though, you should feel that you can go back to your doctor and discuss your progress and any worries you may have at any time. Remember, the doctor is there to help and will understand how frightening depression can be for you.

Mandy became depressed soon after her husband left her for another woman who they had both worked for. Six months previously she had been made redundant by this woman but her husband, who did an identical job, was kept on, along with five others – only she lost her job. At the time she had been very upset and could not understand why her husband had not been angry on her behalf, especially as they needed the money. Only when her husband left did she find out that the affair had been going on for two years and her not being in the same office made it easier for them to be together more often. Four weeks after his departure he said he did not want to sell their house; as they did not have any children she would have to move out, or he would borrow the money to pay off her share and he would move the other woman in. Mandy went to see her doctor in sheer desperation. She had no job, no money and the threat of losing her home hanging over her head. The doctor put her on antidepressants, but she felt sick and drowsy for the first week and stopped taking them because she said they made her feel worse. A month later she was back at her doctor's surgery even more depressed than ever. This time she saw a doctor who explained about the way antidepressants needed time to work and together they looked at the side-effects of different tablets. Mandy agreed to go back on to the treatment but this time on a different type of drug which caused her no problems. Ten months on she was feeling much better, had filed for a divorce and had a part-time job, and her solicitor was trying to secure the house, which she was still living in, for her. She was also being encouraged by her solicitor and work colleagues to go to an industrial tribunal for unfair dismissal, on the grounds that her employer sacked her to get her out of the way so she could have an affair with her husband.

If you are to take antidepressants it is important that you understand how they are going to help you. Making yourself part of your healing process is far better than feeling like just another person who has been handed a prescription and sent away to see what happens. Sometimes the doctor is too busy to explain things; other times the patient is not really well enough to ask the questions that they need to. If you feel this is the case with you either make a list of questions before you visit the doctor or ask a friend or relative to go with you for support. There is a far better chance of a speedier recovery if there is a working partnership between the patient and the doctor right from the beginning. Do not be afraid to make notes each time you visit the doctor. We all know the feeling of getting home and being unable to remember what was said.

So now let us look at how antidepressants work. Depression can be caused by many problems, as we have discussed in previous chapters, and is a disagreeable experience that many people face in their lives. When this happens and we get depressed other biological changes take place in our bodies, and these produce the symptoms that are often presented to the doctor, such as sadness, fatigue, difficulty in sleeping and concentration and a general lack of interest in things around us. When depression occurs it is thought it could be caused by the natural chemicals in the brain, either noradrenaline or serotonin or both, becoming under-active.

Whatever antidepressant you take will work by increasing the levels of these chemicals in the brain. So, you see, depression is like any other illness; it is not imaginary or a weakness. It is just as important that you take the medication if your doctor prescribes it as it is for any other ailment. If you are having difficulty accepting this tell yourself that talking about the way you feel may help the problems and taking the tablets may help the symptoms. The results are good and so are your chances of a full recovery. Research has shown that if 100 people with depression are all given an antidepressant, about 70 will make a good recovery. If one medication does not work for you it is definitely a case of trying another until you find the one that does.

Let us now look at different types of antidepressants that are available.

How many different types are there?

There are several different groups available in the UK. Look at Figure 6, which lists those most commonly used.

Figure 6

Antidepressant type	Some examples	Trade name	Are they commonly used?	Are they cheap or expensive?
Tricyclic antidepressants (called TCAs)	Amitriptyline	Tryptizol	Yes	Cheap
	Clomipramine	Anafranil	Yes	Cheap
	Dothiepin	Prothiaden	Yes	Cheap
	Imipramine	Tofranil	No	Cheap
	Lofepramine	Gamanil	Yes	More expensive
Selective serotonin reuptake inhibitors (SSRIs)	Citalopram	Cipramil	No	Expensive
	Fluoxetine	Prozac	Yes	Expensive
	Paroxetine	Seroxat	Yes	Expensive
	Sertraline	Lustral	Yes	Expensive
Monoamine oxidase inhibitors (MAOIs)	Phenelzine	Nardil	No	Cheap
	Tranylcypromine	Parnate	No	Cheap
Serotonin and noradrenaline reuptake inhibitor (SNRI)	Venlafaxine	Efexor	No	Expensive

Let's look in more detail at the different types of antidepressants.

Tricyclic antidepressants (pronounced try-sye-click) also called TCAs

There are about 15 tricyclic antidepressants; four of them account for most prescriptions for TCAs. These are amitriptyline, clomipramine, dothiepin and lofepramine.

What exactly are they?

They are a group of antidepressants that have been around for over 30 years. They are effective in treating depression and are also sometimes used for other reasons, like pain relief, for treatment of anxiety and to help people sleep. Millions of people have taken antidepressants and have recovered from depression using them.

Are TCAs safe to take?

They are safe to take in the prescribed dose, but they don't suit everyone. There are some conditions where TCAs are best avoided. You should tell your doctor if any of the following apply to you.

1 If you have illnesses such as:

- epilepsy;
- diabetes;
- glaucoma;
- heart complaints;
- liver problems;
- kidney problems;
- prostate trouble.

2 If you are taking other medication from your chemist, especially antihistamines like Triludan (terfenadine), Hismanal (astemizole) and a medicine for stomach acid called Tagamet (cimetidine).
3 If you are pregnant or breast-feeding or are trying for a baby.

TCAs are dangerous if you take an overdose. If you do take one, or suspect that someone has taken one, dial 999 immediately. Tell the doctors what drug has been taken – this is important. The antidote is a glass of what is called 'activated charcoal', but it needs to be taken soon afterwards. Activated charcoal reduces the amount of the drug absorbed into the body.

How should I take TCAs?

Look at your medicine bottle or packet. Follow the doctor's instructions carefully. Take your dose with a full glass of water. Never change the dose itself – always ask your doctor or pharmacist if you're not sure what the dose is.

What if I miss a dose?

Don't worry. Take it as soon as you remember, as long as it is only a few hours after the usual time. Otherwise, wait until your next dose is due and take it as usual – don't try to catch up by doubling your next dose.

How soon can I expect it to work?

Any insomnia should improve within a few days, though you probably won't notice any difference in your mood for a few weeks – but keep going. You'll have good days and bad days, but this is normal. Eventually, you will have more and more good days – just give your medication time to work.

What side-effects happen with TCAs?

Look at Figure 7: it tells you about some of the common side-effects that happen with TCAs. Don't worry if you don't get them. If you do get them, they are often mild and gradually go away.

Figure 7

Side-effect	What it means	What can I do about it?
Sedation	Feeling sleepy or drowsy It can last for a few hours after taking your dose	Don't drive or use machinery Ask a doctor if you can take your medication at bed-time
Constipation	Feeling 'bunged up' Difficulty in passing motion	Eat more fibre and fruit Drink plenty of fluids If it's bad, ask your doctor or chemist for a laxative
Dry mouth	Not much saliva or spit	Suck sugar-free sweets, or chew sugar-free gum If it's bad, you can get a mouth spray from your doctor
Blurred vision	Things look hazy and you can't focus properly	Don't drive You don't need glasses See your doctor if you are worried

---

Can I take alcohol with TCAs?

Taking alcohol with TCAs can make you feel very drowsy. Drinking alcohol, even in moderation, can delay or reduce your response to antidepressants, so it's best avoided. However, don't stop taking your medication if you fancy a drink at the weekend, just be careful and limit it to only one drink.

What about driving?

TCAs can affect your ability to concentrate and react quickly in emergency situations, so you should not drive. You also need to be careful in other situations where accidents could happen – especially at home, in the kitchen, on the stairs, or doing DIY.

What if I've got any more questions?

Ask your doctor or pharmacist for information about your particular medication.

Selective serotonin reuptake inhibitors (also called SSRIs for short)

There are five SSRIs and one similar antidepressant.
These SSRIs are:

- citalopram;
- fluoxetine;
- fluvoxamine;
- paroxetine;
- sertraline.

The similar antidepressant is called nefazodone, trade name: Dutonin.

What exactly are they?

The SSRIs are among the latest antidepressants and have been available in the UK since 1988. The most recent one – citalopram – became available in 1995. They are effective in treating depression and are sometimes used for other reasons, like treatment of anxiety or panic and some eating disorders like anorexia, where people avoid eating, or bulimia, where people binge and then make themselves vomit. They are widely used and millions of people have taken them and have recovered from depression using them.

Are SSRIs safe to take?

They are safe to take in the prescribed dose, but don't suit everyone. There are some conditions where you need to take extra care, so if any of the following apply to you, get in touch with your doctor.

1 If you have illnesses such as:

- epilepsy;
- diabetes;
- liver trouble;
- kidney trouble.

2 If you are taking other medication, including medication from your chemist, especially:

- theophylline (for asthma);
- warfarin (following a stroke).

3 If you are pregnant or breast-feeding or trying for a baby.

How should I take SSRIs?

Look at your medicine bottle or packet. Follow the doctor's instructions carefully. Take your dose with a full glass of water. Never change the dose itself – always ask your doctor or pharmacist if you're not sure what the dose is.

What if I miss a dose?

Don't worry. Take it as soon as you remember, as long as it is only a few hours after the usual time. Otherwise, wait until your next dose is due to take it as usual – don't try to catch up by doubling your next dose.

How soon can I expect it to work?

If you have been experiencing insomnia, you should find that sleep improves within a few days, though you probably won't notice any difference in your mood for a few weeks – but keep going. You'll have good days and bad days, but this is normal. Eventually, you will have more and more good days – just give your medication time to work.

What side-effects happen with SSRIs

Look at Figure 8: it tells you about some of the common side-effects that happen with SSRIs. Don't worry if you don't get them. If you do get them, they are often mild and gradually go away.

Figure 8

Side-effect	What it means	What can I do about it?
Nausea	Feeling sick Sometimes being sick	Take your medication after food If you are sick for more than a day consult your doctor
Insomnia	Not being able to get to sleep at night	This can also be a symptom of depression Discuss with your doctor Change the time of your dose to morning
Sedation	Feeling sleepy or drowsy It can last for a few hours after taking your dose	Don't drive or use machinery Ask a doctor if you can take your medication at bed-time
Headache	Painful pounding feeling in your head	Ask your chemist if it's safe to take aspirin or paracetamol
Restlessness	Feeling tense and nervous You may sweat more	Try to relax, take deep breaths Wear loose clothing
Sexual dysfunction	Finding it hard to have an orgasm – to 'come' No desire for sex	Discuss with your doctor.

Can I take alcohol with SSRIs?

Taking alcohol with SSRIs can make you feel very drowsy. Drinking alcohol, even in moderation, can delay or reduce your response to antidepressants, so it's best avoided. However, don't stop taking your medication if you fancy a drink at the weekend, just be careful and limit it to only one drink.

What about driving?

SSRIs do not usually affect your ability to drive.

What if I've got any more questions?

Ask your doctor or pharmacist for information about your particular medication.

Monoamine oxidase inhibitors (called MAOIs for short)

There are 3 MAOIs and one similar antidepressant.
  The MAOIs are:

- isocarboxazid (Marplan)
- phenelzine (Nardil)
- tranylcypromine (Parnate)

The similar antidepressant is called moclobemide (Manerix). Moclobemide is a 'reversible inhibitor of monoamine oxidase – A' or a RIMA.

What exactly are they?

These are antidepressants that work by deactivating an enzyme called monoamine oxidase. The MAOIs have been around for about 30 years and are effective for all types of depression, including depression with unusual symptoms and depression where other antidepressants have not worked well. Thousands of people with depression have taken them and have recovered using them. They are not widely used because they have a reaction with certain foods.
  Moclobemide has not been around for as long as the MAOIs and, although it works in a similar way, does not usually cause the same problems with some types of food.

Are these safe to take?

They are safe to take in the prescribed dose, but they don't suit everyone. There are some conditions where they should not normally be used. If any of the following apply to you, tell your doctor.

1 If you have illnesses such as:

- diabetes;
- epilepsy;
- overactive thyroid (hyperthyroidism);
- heart trouble;
- liver trouble;
- a condition called phaeochromocytoma.

2 If you are taking medicines, especially those for coughs and colds which you can get without a prescription – see 'medicines to avoid', p. 71.

3 If you are pregnant, breast-feeding or trying for a baby.

How should I take MAOIs?

Look at your medicine bottle or packet. Follow the doctor's instructions carefully. Take your dose with a full glass of water. Never change the dose itself – always ask your doctor or pharmacist if you're not sure what the dose is.

What if I miss a dose?

Don't worry. Take it as soon as you remember, as long as it is only a few hours after the usual time. Otherwise, wait until your next dose is due and take it as usual – don't try to catch up by doubling your next dose.

How soon can I expect it to work?

Any insomnia should improve within a few days, though you probably won't notice any difference in your mood for a few weeks – but keep going. You'll have good days and bad days, but this is normal. Eventually, you will have more and more good days – just give your medication time to work.

What about the foods and medicines I need to avoid?

Some foods contain a naturally occurring chemical called tyramine. Your body uses this to help control your blood pressure. If you mix tyramine with MAOIs, your blood pressure can rise very suddenly and you may feel hot or flushed or have a headache. This can be dangerous. Your chemist will usually give you a card with foods and drinks to avoid. They include:

- broad bean pods;
- cheese;
- chianti wine;
- game;
- home-brewed beer;
- paté;
- pickled herring;
- yeast extracts (Oxo, Marmite, Bovril, Twiglets).

The medicines you need to avoid are those for coughs, colds and flu and strong painkillers such as pethidine. Always ask your chemist or doctor before you buy any of these medicines. The chemist can give you a card with a list of medicines to avoid.

What side-effects can I expect with MAOIs?

Look at Figure 9: it tells you about some of the common side-effects that happen with MAOIs. Don't worry if you don't get them. If you do get them, they are often mild and gradually go away.

Figure 9

Side-effect	What it means	What can I do about it?
Postural hypotension	Feeling dizzy or faint when you get up	Don't stand up quickly If you feel dizzy, don't drive
Sedation	Feeling sleepy in the daytime	Don't drive or use machinery
Constipation	Feeling 'bunged up' Difficulty in passing motion	Eat more fibre and fruit Drink plenty of fluids If it's bad, ask your doctor or chemist for a laxative
Dry mouth	Not much saliva or spit	Suck sugar-free sweets, or chew sugar-free gum If it's bad, you can get a mouth spray from your doctor

---

Can I take alcohol with MAOIs?

Taking alcohol with MAOIs can make you feel very drowsy. Drinking alcohol, even in moderation, can delay or reduce your response to antidepressants, so it's best avoided. However, don't stop taking your medication if you fancy a drink at the weekend, just be careful and limit it to only one drink.

What about driving?

MAOIs can affect your ability to concentrate and react quickly in emergency situations, so you should not drive. You also need to be careful in other situations where accidents could happen – especially at home, in the kitchen, on the stairs, or doing DIY.

Other antidepressants available in the UK

Venlafaxine

An antidepressant made available recently is venlafaxine (Efexor). Venlafaxine is as effective as other antidepressants and may be more effective in some people who have not done well on other antidepressants.

The general information about SSRI antidepressants also applies to venlafaxine.

Side-effects are similar to those of SSRI antidepressants, with the addition of dry mouth and dizziness. In higher doses it can reduce your blood pressure.

Tryptophan

Tryptophan (Optimax) is a naturally occurring chemical which we all take in small quantities in our diet. In larger doses it has been found to benefit some patients who have not done well on antidepressants alone.

In the past, it has been linked to a serious side-effect which affects your blood, so it is now only available for patients not responding to other treatments, who must have blood tests while taking this medication.

Side-effects include drowsiness, nausea, headache and light-headedness.

Flupenthixol

Flupenthixol (Fluanxol, Depoixol) is a major tranquillizer which also acts as an antidepressant. It is used in doses of 1–3 mg daily and may be added to boost the activity of an antidepressant.

Side-effects include: restlessness, insomnia, dizziness, tremor, muscle weakness, muscle stiffness and, in some people, symptoms similar to those of Parkinson's Disease.

Edronax

Edronax (Reboxetine) belongs to a group of antidepressants called NARIs (noradrenaline reuptake inhibitors). This antidepressant is particularly helpful for those suffering from depression accompanied by loss of motivation and energy. As such it is useful because of being so noradrenaline specific. It is to be hoped that the introduction of medicines like this will help to tease out the contribution of different neurotransmitter 'go-betweens' in the field of depression in general and in particular individuals. Unlike the MAOIs (or RIMAs such as moclobemide at higher doses) there are no dietary restrictions. It can cause sleeplessness, nausea or difficulty in urination.

Zispin

Zispin (Mirtazepine) belongs to the group called NASSAs (noradrenergic and specific serotonergic antidepressant) and exerts its effects by increasing levels of both serotonin and noradrenaline. Its main side-effects are sedation and weight gain. It can also cause a drop in the number of white blood cells, and so any persisting sore throat should prompt your doctor to do a blood test.

Antidepressants not included in this list

If you are taking an antidepressant not included in this list, don't worry. Ask your pharmacist or doctor for information.

Antidepressants need to be tailored to meet the needs of individual patients, so if you are not on a commonly prescribed antidepressant, it's probably just because they haven't suited you, while the less common one works for you.

'I finally saw the light at the end of the tunnel' were the words that started Ben's letter to me after he had been taking antidepressants for three months. For the first time since he left his job he found there was not that heavy feeling of gloom weighing him down when he woke up each morning. His night-time panics and lying awake for hours had also disappeared and he had begun to feel he was getting back to his old self again. It had taken him months to seek help from his GP, mainly because his brother and parents had told him he would be hooked for life if he went on antidepressants. Despite their disapproval he finally took the doctor's advice and started taking Prozac. Feeling much better, he was immediately under pressure from his father, who saw depression as a weakness, to come off the tablets and so he did. The result was he slipped back and the depression returned, this time much worse.

Nardia also stopped taking the tablets as soon as she started to feel better, partly because she needed to return to work and did not want her employer to find out that she was on medication, but also because her husband was getting cross because she had no desire for sex and could not get an orgasm, which was one of the side-effects of the tablets she was taking.

In both of these cases, stopping the medication too soon meant even longer off work and recovering. If you have been taking antidepressants you should not come off them until your doctor advises you to do so. Remember, they are not addictive but you need to allow time for the brain chemicals to fully recover. This takes at least four to six months in most people and sometimes even longer. When you agree with your doctor that it is time to stop he will work out a pattern for you to follow so that you can do so without setting yourself back.

There may be many questions that you still need answering regarding your medication, and if this is the case speak to your doctor or your pharmacist. People often say to me, 'I don't like to bother my doctor because he is so busy.' Yes, he may be, but that doesn't mean that you cannot get the reassurance you need. Telephone and ask the receptionist when would be the best time to come in for a chat. Alternatively you may find your doctor has a period in the day when you can speak to him on the phone rather than go to the surgery. It will help if you make a list of questions you need to ask before speaking to him and, as I said before, do not be afraid to make notes of what he says. It is often hard to be able to recognize when you are making any progress – in fact, more people are likely to think they are not than those who think they are. What you have to keep reminding yourself is that you must not put yourself under any pressure to do too much too soon. Small steady steps are better than trying to take great leaps and slipping back.

To help you monitor your progress I would recommend you keeping a wall chart or a diary. I am not going to ask you to laboriously write about it because that would just put more pressure on you; instead, use a star system. Buy yourself a pack of some colourful gummed stars and use these to give yourself a pat on the back each time that you do something that you enjoy or feel good about. Divide your chart into days and sections like the one in Figure 10, and boost your confidence as each star gets stuck on. Yes, it might take you back to your childhood days when you got stars for good work or behaviour, but that does not matter. I started to learn the piano a while ago and could not wait to show my children my silver star which I got for the first time I managed to play 'Jingle Bells' (rather jerkily, I might add) all the way through for my piano teacher. We all need encouragement sometimes, and we have to give it to ourselves as well as getting it from others. It's not vain or self-satisfied – it is about learning to value yourself, and when you are depressed this is a very important lesson to learn. Do not expect too much of yourself or get down if there are some days when you do less than others. When you were well you accepted without question that every day varied; now is no different.

This is only a guide: you can give yourself stars for anything. If you want to use different colours you can denote how well you felt you did, but don't do this if it gets you agitated as soon as it takes more thought. You can make your chart out of any paper, but the cheapest and easiest is probably on a sheet of wallpaper. If your family will join in and encourage you then the kitchen might well be a good place for it. If you prefer it to be more private then choose a place where it is not going to be seen by everyone or do it in the front of your diary.

Depression affects the quality of your life and those around you. Taking antidepressants could be an effective form of treatment that will set you on the road to recovery. If you had broken a leg, had diabetes, cancer or any other illness you would not think twice about taking medication. Depression is no different. Millions of people have faced the same feelings that you have now, but antidepressants have helped them to look forward to a happy future and there is every reason to trust that this will happen for you very soon.

Figure 10

I am getting there!

Tasks	Mon	Tue	Wed	Thu	Fri	Sat	Sun	Mon	Tue	Wed	Thu	Fri	Sat	Sun	Mon
Got up		*		*	*	*	*	*	*		*		*	*	*
Had a wash				*	*	*		*					*	*	*
Got dressed			*					*					*	*	*
Remembered to take tablets	*	*	*	*	*	*	*	*	*	*	*	*	*	*	*
Had breakfast												*	*	*	
Went for a walk											*				*
Read a book															
Listened to music													*	*	
Watched TV	*		*					*					*	*	
Had lunch			*		*	*	*	*							*

WILL I BECOME AN ADDICT IF I TAKE ANTIDEPRESSANTS?

Made a phone call				*		*	
Went to the shops				*		*	
Talked to the family		*					
Wrote a letter							
Read the paper	*						
Had supper	*						
Visited friends							
Had a visitor			*		*	*	
Enjoyed having a visitor						*	
Slept most of the night				*		*	*
Felt more positive today							*
Set myself a goal				*			*
Managed to reach goal							*

8

'Can I Help Myself?'
Taking Control of Your Life!

When Debbie became depressed and had to go on to antidepressants she felt her life had been taken over not only by the illness but also by the medication. She knew the tablets were beginning to have a beneficial effect but that still didn't take away the feeling that she was no longer in charge of her own destiny. Family, friends and colleagues were all being understanding, and even the children at the nursery school where she worked seemed to be on their best behaviour for her, as if they knew she was unwell. At one time she had thought she would have to give up the job that she loved. Differences between her and the woman who owned the nursery school seemed to cast a shadow over her whole life, yet when she became depressed and talked about leaving it was the same woman who told her she was needed and not to get herself into such a state every time they disagreed over things. She suggested that Debbie should take up yoga and try to relax. Debbie took her advice and found she looked forward to her yoga class; it did help her to feel relaxed and in charge of her life once again. Maybe this is something that might help you too.

Antidepressants can work wonders but, like Debbie, many people want to feel they have a hand in their own recovery. In this chapter we are going to look at many ways that you can do this. Not everything will suit you but I am sure you will be able to find something that does.

One of the things many depressed people complain about is their inability to relax, so let's look at this first. When we are feeling low or stressed the mind goes into a world of its own. Someone once described it to me as feeling that their head didn't belong to them any more: it seemed to have a will of its own and caused a heavy feeling across the shoulders. I think that's a very good description. When this happens either the mind races, making you on edge all the time, or it becomes slower and befuddled and unable to concentrate. Sleep problems are often aggravated by the inability to relax, and that is why it is imperative to make sure that you are relaxed before you try to go to sleep.

Start by taking a look at your bedroom. Make sure it is warm and cosy, that your bed is comfortable, that you like the way the room is laid out and that the lighting is right for you. If it is noisy see what you can do to overcome this – perhaps having secondary double glazing could be a good investment.

If you eat too much or too late this can stop you sleeping. If you are hungry this may cause you to wake up early. Try to cut down on alcohol and drinks with caffeine, such as tea and coffee, during the evening as they can disturb your sleep pattern as well. Alcohol may help you to get off to sleep but it is almost certain that you will wake up in the night because of it.

There is nothing worse than going to bed with a troubled mind. If you are worried about something write it down on a piece of paper and tell yourself that you will deal with it tomorrow. In the light of day problems don't seem so bad.

Have a warm bath before you go to bed. Providing you are careful and have candles in safe jars or containers, a candlelit bath with soft music in the background will put you in the right frame of mind for the relaxation exercises that follow. Get yourself settled comfortably in bed and do the relaxation of the body exercises first, followed by the ones for the mind.

Relaxation of the body and mind

Relaxation – body

1 Sit or lie comfortably.
2 Close eyes gently. Become aware of your body and how it feels.
3 Tighten the muscles in your feet. Be aware of how it feels. Slowly let the tension go. Let your feet feel relaxed and heavy.
4 Using this technique of tightening and relaxing, continue up the body, starting with the calf, then the thigh. Then use the method on buttocks, abdomen, back, chest, shoulders, then hands, lower and upper arms, neck and face.
5 When your whole body is relaxed become aware of your breathing again. Relax your whole body further. Lie quietly for several minutes. When ready slowly bring your body back to a state of readiness. Open your eyes while lying down. Do not sit up until you are quite ready.

Relaxation – mind

1 Sit or lie comfortably.
2 Close eyes gently.
3 Relax all your muscles as with the exercises for the body, from feet to face.
4 Breathe through your nose and listen to your breathing.
5 Repeat the word 'one' or any other sound that you choose for this purpose. This will help you relax further.
6 Continue for 10 to 20 minutes. Do not use an alarm. You will soon learn to judge time naturally. At the end, let yourself become gradually aware of your surroundings. Sit quietly for a while before getting up.

During your relaxation time, do not try and force yourself to be relaxed. This will come naturally and with practice. Let any distracting thoughts flow through your mind rather than trying to banish them. Gently bring your word or thought back in. Most benefit is achieved by practising twice a day, but not too soon after a meal.

If you do these every night and at some point during the morning, again lying on the bed, within a couple of weeks you should start to notice an improvement in the way you feel and your sleep pattern. If you can't lie down sit in a comfortable chair, preferably with your feet propped up.

Some people will be offered a chance to have counselling when they are depressed, and it is something that is well worth trying. Contrary to what people think the counsellor will not tell you what to do. Counselling is about talking about your life and seeing what can be done to make it happier. The counsellor is there to help the client to look at their problem areas and the options open to them, and to make any choices or changes that they feel will help them to get on with their life.

Meditation is another way of bringing an element of calm into your life. It takes practice to perfect but, whether you choose modern or more traditional meditation, once you start you will find it can make an immense difference to your life. Although there are many books available on the subject it is possible to join a meditation group rather than learning alone.

Patricia Carrington, PhD, who wrote *The Book of Meditation* (Element, 1998), describes meditation as a grace that releases people from negative behaviours. She says that when people have the opportunity to tune in to their true selves through meditation an overwhelming majority of these people become more patient, compassionate and softer human beings. She goes on to describe meditation as 'a simple gentler method which has a profound gift for humanity which if recognised and used wisely can result in a new flowering of the human spirit'. Certainly it is something that gives hope to many people who are trying to help themselves overcome depression.

Personally I have always favoured visualization as a good way of relaxing and getting healing. It is simple to do once you get the hang of it. You need to sit or lie in a comfortable position. Some people like to do visualization in a completely quiet room but I find it more relaxing to have some quiet gentle music playing in the background. There are many different kinds of visualization. Here are two for you to try, but you can imagine your own.

Close your eyes and imagine you are in a beautiful garden. Everything is peaceful, the sun's warm rays are shining. You are wearing a long white silk robe which is soft to the touch. In your mind walk around the garden, taking in its beauty. Take your time – there is no rush. Eventually you come to some white marble steps that lead down to the most beautiful blue pool you have ever seen. Walk down the steps, slip off your robe and walk into the pool. The water is warm yet refreshing, and you know that it is healing you. Stay in for as long as you want and then slowly leave. You will see a pile of thick fluffy warm towels by the pool. Wrap yourself up in these and then go back up the steps and let the sun's rays pour down on you, cleansing your mind and body. Gradually bring yourself back to the room where you are sitting or lying and listen to the music for a little bit longer, and then gradually open your eyes. Don't rush to get up; give yourself time and relax.

In the second visualization you have to choose where you want to be. Once again listen to the music or perhaps a tape of sounds of the sea or the countryside, depending on where you choose. Relax and imagine you are standing or sitting in a field; the sun is shining and a gentle breeze is swaying the grass, which is strewn with red poppies. Through the field is a path that leads to the gate. Go along the path and through the gate. This leads you to where you want to be – perhaps a beach, a church, the hills, a favourite house, anywhere that makes you feel safe and happy. Stay in this place in your mind and soak up the feelings of peace and tranquillity that it offers. When you are ready to leave, go back through the gate and along the path, and lie or sit in the field again. Gradually become aware of your room, and after a few minutes, open your eyes and lie still for a while before getting up.

Visualization is a good way of relaxing and helping yourself. You may not find it that easy to do to begin with, but with practice you will be able to master it and derive its benefits.

The shelves of supermarkets and chemists offer a wide range of aromatherapy oils, candles and bath essences, made from the most natural of ingredients. Many people have found aromatherapy very instrumental in helping them when they are depressed, and find these products help relaxation, reduce stress and aid sleep.

There are those who decide that they want to have healing, and there is nothing wrong with this so long as you make sure that the healer you choose is reputable, preferably recommended, and that you don't part with huge amounts of money to get this. Many healers don't charge for their healing sessions, which they see as a gift that they have to share. Others do charge, but only a small amount. This is something you have to judge for yourself, both in cost and what you feel you are receiving from it.

For those who prefer to have a type of therapy that is supported by a therapist but one that you can still practise on your own, cognitive therapy could be the answer. Your GP will be able to advise whether a cognitive therapist is available in your area. Cognitive therapy is an effective treatment for depression which is based on the idea that how you think largely determines the way you feel. Cognitive therapy is not just another method of positive thinking. It enables you to recognize and challenge upsetitng thoughts. By challenging negative thoughts it makes you feel better and helps you to think more realistically.

When you are depressed the way you think and your moods change; you tend to look on the bad side of everything and see the worst in yourself, and can see no hope for the future.

Look at the following and see if you have any of these negative thoughts.

- I am useless.
- I am unlovable.
- My partner doesn't love me any more.

- My marriage is a failure.
- I am useless at my job.
- I always mess things up.
- No one likes me.
- I am a waste of space.

Thoughts like these are called negative automatic thoughts because they come into your mind without you wanting them to. Although they may seem convincing, they are distorted and don't fit the facts.

We all have negative thoughts, but when we are well we have twice as many positive ones to negative thoughts. When we are depressed the negative thoughts push all the positive ones away. Everything seems pointless. Depression is perpetuated by negative thoughts. It's a bit like a chicken and egg situation. You may think to yourself, 'No one has phoned me recently ... that must mean nobody likes me ... I am no good, I won't ever have any friends.' You then have depressed feelings which in turn stop you contacting friends, you refuse invitations and you avoid people. Then the circle starts again, with you feeling even more sure that people now hate you.

It's easy when you are depressed to interpret things in the worst possible light. You stop doing things because of these negative gloomy thoughts and this makes you feel even worse. The fact that your friend didn't phone because they had been ill or had to work late isn't an option you will even consider, and so the vicious circle continues. Cognitive therapy helps you recognize how your thoughts, attitudes, beliefs and assumptions affect the way you feel.

It teaches you to question whether your automatic negative thoughts really fit the facts and how to replace them with more realistic ones. It is a proven way of changing your behaviour that is keeping you trapped in your depression.

Cognitive therapists encourage their clients to act like scientists towards their thoughts, not to take negative thoughts for granted but instead to put them under the microscope and weigh up the evidence for and against them. Like anything it takes time: you won't succeed overnight, but this process of challenging thoughts is a skill that can be learnt and used to help you overcome your depression.

This is only a brief glimpse into cognitive therapy based on thoughts, feelings and behaviour, but it is one that an increasing number of depressed people are finding works for them.

Ask yourself if you are jumping to the wrong conclusions.
Keep a cognitive diary like the one in Figure 11.

Figure 11

Date	Situation	Feelings	Negative thoughts
1 March	My car wouldn't start	Frustrated and down	Nothing goes right for me I am useless
2 March	Mum phoned to say she was going to visit my brother	Miserable, lonely	She doesn't want to be with me, she obviously doesn't love me I hate myself
4 March	Jane cancelled meeting me for lunch today	Depressed, unhappy	Why would anyone want to see me? Other people are more interesting than me I am boring
5 March	Didn't get any overtime at work today	Inadequate, useless	The world would be a better place without me Why doesn't anything go right for me? I will probably get the sack from my job

---

This will enable you to see if you are having negative automatic
thoughts. If you are, then using cognitive techniques will help you
recover, so speak to your GP.

Some people will decide that they need to find the cause of their
depression rather than just treat the symptoms, and choose to do this
with hypnotherapy, while others will try acupuncture, reflexology or
one of many other alternative therapies available. It is entirely up to
you what you choose, but it's a good idea to let your doctor know
what you are doing.

Surroundings make an awful lot of difference to our lives. Little
touches can go a long way to make our home or place of work nicer.
Comfortable seating, good lighting, pictures, flowers, family photos,

holiday souvenirs will all give you a feeling of being among things that you care about, which in turn makes you feel better about yourself.

Today there is no reason to cope alone when you are depressed. Apart from family and friends there are many excellent organizations that offer advice, information and support.

One of these is Depression Alliance, who offer support through an excellent network of self-help groups throughout the United Kingdom. People with depression meet together and give each other support. This helps to dispel the feeling that you are suffering alone. One member of Depression Alliance told me, 'It was such a relief to talk to other people who were feeling exactly the same as me. I thought I was rubbish because I was depressed but now I know I am not. I am no different from the others at the group, who are all nice people but unwell.'

Depression Alliance also offer a wide range of information publications, a pen-friend scheme and a newsletter called 'Single Step' which members can contribute to. Many members find this newsletter very reassuring, knowing that Depression Alliance is there to support them. Depression Alliance also have a website on www.depressionalliance.org which gives details of the work that Depression Alliance does, plus an up-to-date list of all groups across the country. If you prefer to write to them, their address is Depression Alliance, 35 Westminster Bridge Road, London, SE1 7JB.

The largest and probably best-known mental health charity in England and Wales is MIND. They have branches all over the UK for people with all kinds of mental illness, offering counselling, befriending and day centres where people can participate in a wide range of activities. They work tirelessly to reduce the stigma of depression and are well respected and listened to, both nationally and in the local community.

For those of you who are on the Internet you may be interested to know that the Royal College of Psychiatrists now has a very user-friendly website on depression in the workplace (which can be accessed on www.rcpsych.ac.uk).

Finally we must not forget the Samaritans, who offer a listening ear 24 hours a day, 365 days of the year. No matter how large or small your problem, they are always just a phone call away and can offer the chance to talk through your worries rather than feeling you are alone. Their number is 0845 790 90 90.

Some of you may choose to go for a relaxing massage, to a concert, swimming or for a walk. It doesn't matter what you choose. The important thing is that you are taking control of your life.

No one method of self-help will suit everyone, but taking time for yourself will go a long way to helping you overcome your depression. Self-help should be used in conjunction with the treatment that your doctor has prescribed. These self-help therapies empower people so that they can get on with their lives. Used to complement the treatment that your doctor has described they can speed up recovery and give you a real sense of achievement.

Questions and answers

Q I joined a self-help group for people who are depressed thinking that it would make me feel better, but it doesn't. Everyone else says how wonderful it is to be with others who feel the same but I find it terrifying. I am forcing myself to attend these meetings but I feel better when I don't go ... relieved!
A Then don't go. What suits one person won't be right for another. I understand exactly how you feel. When I had cancer I went along to a cancer self-help group and found myself feeling exactly as you do. It made me feel trapped, so I stopped going and haven't looked back since. Most people find these groups a lifeline, but there will always be those like you and me who cope better on their own. There is nothing wrong with this.

Q I would like to try cognitive therapy but I am worried that it wouldn't work for me because I have always been a negative person, even when well.
A There you go, being negative again – proof that cognitive therapy is just up your street! It's designed to help you have positive thoughts, so make a start and go for it.

Q My office is a mess, clutter everywhere, and I haven't got the energy or the inclination to clear it up. My work partner keeps going on at me to do something about it – he says it creates a bad impression on the staff and clients who visit. The trouble is I feel so depressed lately. We set up the business by mortgaging ourselves up to our necks. Six months ago he was left a house and quite a lot of assets and now he lords it over me all the time. He has paid off his debts, I am still saddled with mine.

A Working among clutter can make your depression even worse. Can you enlist the help of your family or a friend one weekend and blitz the place? I think this would help you to have a more positive attitude towards your work. It's unfair of your partner if he is gloating, but maybe the unfairness of the situation is making you believe this is so when it may not be. So get rid of the clutter and talk to him about the way you feel. You need to get back into a good working relationship again and then I am sure you will start to feel better.

9

Want to Return to Work? Worried? Uncertain?

As your depression recedes and your confidence returns your thoughts may turn to going back to work. This may be for several reasons – guilt that you have not been working or earning, the need to prove to yourself and others that you are back on course or a genuine need to get back into the world of work and be part of it. Just because you think about it doesn't mean that you are ready to do it or even want to. The thinking part is a very important stage because it shows that you are starting to focus on the options open to you, so however you feel about returning to work you can give yourself a pat on the back for getting this far.

If the thought of returning to work fills you with absolute horror then you need to ask yourself the following questions.

- Is the thought of returning to the job you left scaring you?
- Would you feel better about it if you found a different job?
- Would you like to train for something different?
- Would voluntary work with less pressure be a good option before paid work?

You may feel you are not ready for any of these options. If so do not worry; now is not the time to put yourself under more pressure. Just accept that the time is not right yet. One day it will be.

Many people see their period of depression as being a time in their life which has been wasted, but this is totally untrue. Every experience in life teaches us something, and depression is no exception. It has certainly taught you to have an understanding of your strengths and weaknesses, something most people do not have a clue about. It has also equipped you with an understanding that you didn't have before, one that will help you to understand and support colleagues and friends to cope better in difficult situations in the future.

Recognizing the signs of depression in others may not seem of great importance, but it is. Perhaps if someone had seen the warning signs with you and understood what was going on you would not have had to be off work in the first place.

Voluntary work is certainly a good option if you are dithering about going back to work. The work is not any less valuable – in fact much of it will be invaluable – but because there is no payment involved the pressure seems far less. It is also something that gives you plenty of choices; you can pick one area to work in or several.

Voluntary work was what Kevin chose when he didn't feel ready to return to paid employment. Unsure of what he wanted to do, he started by helping to run the League of Friends shop at the local hospital two afternoons a week. He then went on to help run a club for children with problems. Now well into the voluntary sector, he became co-ordinator for the local guild of voluntary services and organized a list of drivers to take people to certain events. Kevin found this offered a good amount of job satisfaction and enough responsibility to make him feel good about himself without too much pressure.

It also gave Kevin the chance to realize that he didn't want to go back to his job as a long-distance lorry driver, that he liked the day-to-day contact with people. The thought of returning to where he had worked for 18 years filled him with dread. But he wanted to get back into paid employment, partly because he hated being on benefits and also because he knew it was a step he had to take if he was to be fully recovered. With no qualifications his options were limited, but after much deliberation Kevin decided to apply for and got a place on an access course at his local college. He hopes to go on to unversity and eventually to get a paid position in the voluntary sector.

Meg also did voluntary work but it wasn't right for her. She felt it didn't give her the self-worth she needed. It did, however, spur her on to look for paid work which she might not have done had she not ventured into voluntary work.

Depression has been described by many people as a watershed in their lives which has enabled them to make changes in their lifestyle. Although a terrible thing to go through, depression often shifts people's insights and goals into a different perspective. Life never looks the same after depression but, believe me, it can seem better.

Retraining might seem a very scary road to take, especially if you have not done any kind of study for years, but for many it is a second chance that they never thought they would get. How many people leave school, college or university and choose a career that they are happy with? The answer to this is, not many. Often it was a case of taking the first job that came along and drifting with it for years. Others find what they want out of life changes as they get older, and this applies to their work as well.

Maybe you have wanted to change direction but financial restraints, family responsibilities or just fear of the unknown have stopped you. Well, now could be the time to reassess your career path and decide if you want to do something different.

It may mean retraining to renew your skills, but this will also give you the chance to develop your confidence and recognize your capabilities.

After a long depressive illness Jacqueline decided she didn't want to go back to her job as a prison officer. She felt the stress of this job and the changes in the work structure and the shift patterns had heavily led to her depression. Although she felt she was well on the road to recovery she recognized that going back to the same job might set her back. Instead she decided to do a GNVQ in leisure and tourism for two years and also to learn French, in the hope that she could get work as a courier with a travel company.

You may say, 'How do I know what is right for me?' So let us look at that next. Depression has given you a chance to review your life, to be open-minded about your future and to value yourself. Start by making a list of what you liked and didn't like about your previous job. Then make a second list of what you would like from your next job and what you would want to avoid. It does not matter how unrealistic this list may appear, it is your baseline to work from and it is up to you to decide what makes a job satisfying for you. A job that makes you feel valued.

Keep this list near to you for reference, for when applying for a job or talking to a former employer if you decide to return to your previous job. To help you decide whether you want to return to your previous job or not I would like you to answer the following 20 questions. There is no pressure, it is not a test, so give it a try and see how you get on. Please tick either yes or no for each question in Figure 12.

Figure 12

	Yes	No
1 Did you get satisfaction from the job you did?	☐	☐
2 Did you get on well with your colleagues?	☐	☐
3 Were the working conditions good?	☐	☐
4 Did you get on with your boss?	☐	☐
5 Did you get support from your colleagues when you became depressed?	☐	☐
6 Was the atmosphere at work happy?	☐	☐
7 Do you blame the job for your depression?	☐	☐
8 Do you feel happy at the prospect of going back to that job?	☐	☐
9 Do you feel you would like a change in your life?	☐	☐
10 Would a new job offer you a fresh start?	☐	☐
11 Is there something new that you would like to try your hand at?	☐	☐
12 Would you be willing to retrain?	☐	☐
13 Is job satisfaction important to you?	☐	☐
14 Do you worry about your health now?	☐	☐
15 Would you enjoy a new challenge?	☐	☐
16 Could you adapt to a new job?	☐	☐
17 Would your family and friends support you whatever you decide to do?	☐	☐
18 Are you open to suggestions?	☐	☐
19 Are you being kind to yourself?	☐	☐
20 Do you think you are ready to return to work?	☐	☐

Answering these questions will give you an indication of what might be right for your future, but do not base any decisions on it just yet.

Repeat the questions several times with a couple of weeks in between and see if you still feel the same. You will probably be surprised to find that you start to answer the questions more decisively each time you do it and that your answers change and develop into a pattern that will eventually help you to make the right choice for you.

Depression is a very lonely experience and one that can stop you from communicating even with those who care. So it is important that you recognize this and discuss your work options with your family and friends and anyone else you trust.

'Discussing' means just that; it does not mean being pressurized into doing anything or letting others make decisions for you. Remember, though, that the longer you leave it the harder it could be, but at the end of the day the decision is yours.

If you have ever been on a diet or tried to stop smoking you will know the 'two steps forward – one step back' syndrome!

It is no different with depression or returning to work. One day it might seem the best idea in the world, the next it could frighten the socks off you. On a good day you may agree to go back to see your employer with a view to returning to work or agree to an interview for another job. Do not be surprised if you feel differently when the day comes. If you cannot face it, don't feel you have let yourself or your family down. Next time you may just make it, so go easy on yourself and accept that it is going to take time. If you broke your leg it would take time to heal. Your mind is no different.

Finding the right job if you decide on a change will take time and planning. This time I am going to let you take the initiative. Make a list of jobs you feel you might enjoy. Think of those that would help you to feel valued, decide on what would make a job satisfying for you. Look at different ways of working, such as part-time, split shifts, shared jobs, temping, working from home and self-employment. One of the things that happens when you suffer with depression is that the structure of your daily routine falls to bits to be replaced by long days where you feel you have done nothing and achieved very little. This in fact is untrue, because every day has a learning curve even though you may not recognize it. The man who didn't get up or the woman who didn't get dressed will see the day as another failure whereas in fact they have been indulging themselves, something they may never have had the chance to do before. Their bodies and minds are saying, 'I can't be bothered to get up today.' Weigh up this against all the hundreds of days that they have worked or looked after the family in the past and they far outweigh this period of depression.

When you begin to think about returning to work it is a good thing to prepare yourself by getting into a daily routine again. I don't mean sticking to a rigid schedule or anything like that: start by deciding what time you would like to get up each day and your mealtimes. Gradually add things like a walk, reading the papers, watching a favourite television programme, going to the shops, visiting the library or seeing friends. Do not rush it, let it happen naturally as you gain confidence.

Reducing stress in other areas of your life will help the process as well. Maybe you took on too many responsibilities at home, never saying no to anyone, and the pressure has piled up and up. Listen to your mind and your body, recognize what you can cope with and what gets you stressed. Keep a simple stress diary so that you can see what triggers stress in your life.

The easiest way to do this is to make a note each day in one or two words as to how you feel; for example 'sad', 'a bit low', 'all right today', 'couldn't cope', 'did well'. When you get a day when you feel particularly stressed put down what you did that day, and, wherever possible what you think caused it.

By doing this you will know what situations are best avoided. You will also start to question yourself, maybe even argue with yourself out loud – not a sign of madness, I hasten to add, but a way of clarifying your ideas and owning them.

You could also ask for additional support from your friends and family at this time. Knowing that you are not alone will go a long way to boost your confidence when you go back to work.

One of the questions I am often asked is, 'Should I tell a potential employer that I have been depressed?' Unfortunately there is no straightforward yes/no answer to this and it is up to each person to decide for themselves. Honesty is always a good basis for any relationship, including a working one, but a stigma about depression exists and some people find it is better only to offer information if directly asked to do so, either verbally or on the application form. Then you should be honest, but make sure you couple this with positive accounts of your recovery and how much you want to return to work. Not telling them the truth might have an adverse effect on the validity of the contract you may have with an employer.

Although you do not want to get yourself wound up before an interview or a meeting with your present employer, it is always a good thing to run through in your mind what you want to say and how you want the interview to go. It is called 'a rehearsal for life'. By thinking it through in a positive way you are getting into the right frame of mind and there will be less anxiety and fear.

There will be things you may want to ask, so do not be afraid to make a list of questions before you go. This will impress the employer and make the chances of getting the job easier.

Check your appearance before you set off, if necessary enlisting the opinion of family or friends. Employers can be forgiven for thinking what they see may be what they get. A dishevelled appearance will make them think you have not got your act together or you can't be bothered. You do not have to look like something out of a tailor's window or off the catwalk, but care with your appearance, even if your clothes are old, will pay off.

If and when you do start back to work, do not work too hard too soon. A steady flow of work is better than a flurry followed by you feeling under pressure and not producing anything.

There could well be a few hiccups along the way, but everyone has problems at work and overcoming them can do wonders for self-confidence. When you do get home from work try to forget it until the next day. Congratulate yourself on what you have achieved rather than looking back and analysing things that you feel you could have done better. Plenty of time for that next day.

Eating properly and keeping your medication up, if that is what you and your doctor have agreed, is essential. Take breaks for drinks, snacks and lunch, and start the day with a breakfast, however small.

We can't leave this subject of returning to work without looking at it from the employer's point of view.

With depression still being at the top of the 'misunderstood' league of illnesses it is little wonder that symptoms go unnoticed. It is my belief that a greater knowledge on the employer's part would increase understanding and reduce the number of people who have to take time off in the first place. Signs to look out for are a change in the employee's usual behaviour – sadness, tears, difficulty concentrating, increased forgetfulness, mistakes, poor time-keeping, irritability, increased absence and an inability to deal with work that they have previously managed all right are just a few.

Over the past few years there seems to have been a widening gap between employers and the workforce, so much so that it would be hard for employers to put their fingers on what may have triggered off the depression in a member of their staff.

Some of the main causes at work include lack of job security, excessive workload, unsociable hours, new responsibilities, poor working environment and repetitive work. This is on top of pressures outside work such as relationship problems, loneliness, money difficulties, illness and bereavement, to name but a few.

Identifying depression triggers, recognizing the signs and being prepared to say, 'Are you all right?' or, 'Can I help?' would make such a difference. In an ideal working world information about depression and easy access to counselling would cut down the number of people who stop work because of it. Thousands and thousands of working hours are lost each year at an enormous cost, not only to the workplace but also for medication and treatment.

Employers need to look at their working environment and ask themselves if it is pleasant or depressing. They need to create an environment with sufficient space, light, heat and ventilation and one where difficulties can be talked about without anyone feeling embarrassed or inadequate. Finally, people who have been depressed should not be underestimated: they have plenty to offer, including a greater understanding than many of their strengths and weaknesses. Through their experience of depression they have learnt a lot and can be a real asset to the workforce.

Questions and answers

Q I have been off work with depression for nearly a year and I am still on antidepressants, but I feel so much better than I did. I am a teacher who found it increasingly difficult to cope with a class of teenagers who seemed to have no interest in learning and only wanted to be as disruptive as they could. I started off getting panic attacks in the middle of difficult lessons, then they came on before lessons as well and this is when the depression set in. It was the summer break, and I thought this would give me time to overcome it. Reluctantly I returned to school at the beginning of the following term, but after two weeks I could not go in any more. Teaching no longer holds the interest that it used to for me but it is all I know. I want to return to work, I teach maths, but how will I face the students, especially as they probably know I have been depressed? This is filling me with despair as I am good at what I do.

A If you have only learnt one thing from the experience of depression it is that you do not enjoy what you are doing any more, so why force yourself to do it? You have years of training and experience . . . so take it elsewhere. Perhaps try a different school, a different age group or even teaching adults, but make this the start of a new phase in your career rather than sticking with one that has made you ill. Nothing is wasted, even the time you have been depressed, as this has given you new insights. Use these constructively and you will not regret it.

Q When my father died my mother became depressed. Up until then she had held down a good job as a supervisor in a factory. To begin with people were sympathetic but this soon wore thin and one of the other supervisors told her she needed to pull herself together as some of the staff were embarrassed when she got upset. She took a month's leave but has not been back since. It is three months now. The silly thing is that the same supervisor now comes and tells her how much everyone is missing her, but Mum is still hanging on to the previous words and says she can't go back in case they think she is a misery. She is much better than she was, and I think going back to work might help her even more.

A There are three issues here, grief over your dad, hurt over what was said, and depressed feelings. Each has to be dealt with, but it has to be in her own time. Your mum's depression is caused by the situation she finds herself in. As she comes to terms with your father's death this should help the depression and help her to accept what the supervisor is now saying. Perhaps if she made a social visit to the factory she would be able to assess everyone's sincerity for herself. It will not be an easy step for her to return to work because it will remind her of painful memories, but if she can do it I think it would help lift her depression.

Q I am scared that my doctor might take me off medication and that I could be forced back to work if my benefits were stopped. I

96

have been off work for six months with depression through having to do the work of three after they made two other people redundant. Each day is difficult to cope with, and I can't see any way out of it. Someone else has my job now; they asked if I was going back and I said that I didn't want to. I told them why but they were not interested. I lie awake at night worrying as I am a 50-year-old single woman living alone with no income other than my benefits and I feel lousy.

A When things are worrying you this much it is best to do something about it. Talk to your doctor, I am sure that if you are as unwell as you say you are no one is going to take you off your tablets or your benefits. But you do have to talk this through. Increased amounts of work are responsible for many people becoming depressed. It sounds as if you have made the right decision to leave this particular job, but do not close your mind to anything else.

Q I am 39, married, with a wife and two small children. I have been off work with depression due to the suicide of a colleague I used to work with. I know he had problems with his partner but I never thought he would kill himself. My employer has been far more understanding than I would have expected and my job is there for me to return to whenever I feel like it. My problem is that I have never enjoyed the work and would prefer to take this opportunity to try and set up my own business. My wife is supportive but she thinks I should go back to my old job as they have been so understanding.

A It is good to hear this, but sometimes we reach watersheds in our lives through unexpected circumstances. If you really want to do this I think you should give it a try. If you do not you will regret it and I am sure your employer, although probably disappointed, will agree and admire you for what you are about to do.

Let me end this chapter by telling you to be kind to yourself. Take each day as it comes and do not expect miracles overnight. You may have bad days, but then everyone does. Believe me, you will survive!

10

The Carers – Friends and Family

When you are depressed it is perfectly understandable to feel angry over what is happening to you and to show that anger to family and friends. It is also very easy to fall into the 'willing victim trap', where you get stuck feeling that no one else can be suffering anything so terrible as you are. The fact that others may lose their jobs, fall upon hard times, be deserted by their partners or even fall ill totally escapes the depressed person, not because they are cold-hearted people but because they find it hard to see beyond the invisible shell that has built up around them, the same one that keeps them locked in a situation from which they desperately want to escape but from which there seems no way out.

Being depressed can make people selfish without their realizing it. Ask someone who is depressed how their wife or husband is and they will almost certainly say, 'Fine, Fine,' when the truth is probably far from this. Try explaining to them that it is a very difficult time for the family as well and their mouths will probably fall open in complete surprise. After all, they are the ones who are depressed, not their family.

I recently had lunch with a couple I have known almost for ever, I will call them John and Mary. The husband is suffering with acute depression and finds life holds very little meaning for him at the moment. Thoughts of wanting to die often cross his mind and although on medication and having counselling he seems to be making very little progress.

Meanwhile his wife, who has seen him through many bouts of depression before, seems to have reached the end of the line herself. She told me how she is worn down by the constant negative thoughts, the having to keep him going on a day-to-day basis and the prospect of having this continuing for a long time ahead. She feels sucked down by all the giving and says she longs for a normal life with a bit of laughter again.

Over lunch we listened to John telling us about his depression, and I did feel very sorry for him. When he is well he is always the one who is the life and soul of the party and contributes so much to the lives of those around him, and I hate to see him so low. Turning the conversation to Mary and asking her how she was feeling and how she was coping I was not at all surprised to see a look of incredulity spread across John's face. After all, wasn't he the one who was suffering, not Mary?

The truth is they are both suffering. You cannot live with someone who is depressed without being affected, and even the kindest, most understanding person has a point where they feel they cannot take much more. For some it may be almost instantaneous; others will support their loved ones over weeks, months or years until they reach saturation point. Many become depressed themselves, often to a point where they are as bad as or even worse than the person they have been looking after.

Depression is something that affects whole families. It can have a particularly bad effect on the children. It scares them to see their mum or dad cry or stare into space for hours on end. I know from when my daughter-in-law was depressed how badly it affected my grandchildren, particularly my grand-daughter. She was confused and scared by her mum's mood swings; this was not how Mummy normally behaved.

It is important that both carers and sufferers are helped to realize that it is not only the depressed person whose life is affected. If you are a sufferer you may feel your life has come to a standstill, but what about those around you? Their lives have to go on as well.

Ask yourself the following questions and try to be honest with your replies.

1 Do you avoid social occasions?
2 Do you dislike having visitors?
3 Would you refuse to go on holiday?
4 Are you letting your partner take on most of the financial and day-to-day responsibilities?
5 Do you hate making decisions?
6 Do you want your own way most of the time?
7 Do you feel like opting out of most of the things you used to do with your friends and family?

If the answer to most of these is 'Yes' and the answer to the following question is 'No' . . .

In all honesty have you thought how your illness is affecting those close to you?

... then maybe your family could be finding life rather more difficult to cope with than you realize.

Perhaps there is anger building up on both sides, in you because you feel so unwell and low, and in your partner and family because, despite loving you, they feel trapped in a 'no win' situation.

One lady called Sally, whose husband Steve was depressed, described it as putting endless coins into a fruit machine and never winning. She loved her husband to bits, but however much she supported and encouraged him he was constantly miserable and dragging her down as well. Unable to cope and feeling it hard to suppress the anger she often felt towards her husband, she had to go on antidepressants herself and was seeing a counsellor. She told me how, before her husband's demotion at work due to restructuring, they had been quite happy. She had a good job at the same company and that had been unaffected by the changes. This had made matters worse; her husband's confidence dwindled, depression set in and he had been off work for nearly nine months.

Friends had suggested she give up her job and take another elsewhere so that it did not rub salt into the wounds each time she went to work, but after counselling and much thought she decided that this was not the right thing to do. Her stability at home was at an all-time low but at least at work she felt safe doing what she was used to. She doubted if giving up her job would help her husband to get better. If anything, it would put more of a strain on their relationship, both emotionally and financially, especially as she loved her job and did not want to leave.

After a lot of encouragement by his doctor Steve eventually agreed to go to counselling, first on his own and then with Sally. Over the next six months he was able to accept that his demotion had nothing whatsoever to do with his ability to do the job, that his job would have disappeared whoever had held it, that restructuring means changes, and that he had allowed jealous feelings towards his wife, because she had kept her job at the company, to drag his self-esteem down even lower.

Today Sally still works at the same company, but Steve took

early retirement at 50 on the grounds of ill health. Since then he has set up his own small consultancy business. Working from home it holds very little financial stress, as Sally is earning and he has a pension. Also he feels he is in charge of his own destiny, he stands or falls on his own merits and he does not feel under threat from anyone.

There are many emotions that carers go through, and one of these is guilt. It is easy to think you could be the cause of your partner's or loved one's depression, especially if you have not been getting on too well. There is also the worry that you are not doing enough to help them on the road to recovery. It is important that carers realize that there are limitations to how much responsibility they can take on. No one can expect to say, 'Here is my life, it is up to you to make me happy.' Support, encouragement, understanding and the ability to listen are the best gifts you can offer. But at the same time you must look after yourself, otherwise there will be no one strong enough to cope with the situation.

One thing carers have to do is to find time for themselves to do the things that they enjoy and have space without feeling guilty about it. This is not easy, especially if it is your partner who is depressed and they do not want to go out and object to your doing so as well. Hard as it may seem, you must be firm and do it. By doing so you will recharge your batteries so that you can cope for the rest of the time.

Some may say it is not worth the effort when they have to put up with the sulks or bad moods both before they go out and when they return, but I believe it is. It reduces the levels of resentment that often build up. However, it must be done in a sensitive way, otherwise the sufferer will be the one who ends up feeling rejected and even more depressed.

Paul and Maureen found themselves having to face up to this situation. When she became depressed, Paul's safety valve was his one night a week playing darts down at his local club. Maureen had never liked him going out on his own and it had been a bone of contention and the subject of many arguments even before she became depressed. Paul worked long hours at the colliery and since his wife became depressed after a row with her supervisor at work, he had found it increasingly difficult to meet up with his pals on a Wednesday night. Maureen would get so upset at being left at home, but she had turned down invitations to go with him. It was Maureen's sister Beryl who finally helped Paul to get his evening out by suggesting that Maureen spent the evening with her and a couple of friends.

Maureen was talked round, and although she would be the last one to admit it she does enjoy her evening out and it is helping her to get over her depression. Each week her sister phones her and gives her the option to meet up or not, so as not to put too much pressure on her. They meet at each other's houses and each brings a part of the meal. Maureen always volunteers to take a bottle of wine even though she does not drink, because this is less effort than having to do some cooking.

Grieving for a depressed person may seem an odd thing but in many ways it is true. It is a kind of sadness and a longing for the person who used to be, the one you used to feel secure and happy with but who now seems to have disappeared. To see someone you love going through the misery of depression and becoming so changed can be a very frightening experience. You need to keep reassuring yourself that that person is still there but at the moment is too scared to reveal themselves. Believe me, one day, just like the sun coming out, they will too.

Fear of the future and what lies ahead is a constant worry for the carer. What makes it even worse is that they feel they have very little control over their situation, yet they often feel they should have. It is a bit like being cast on the sea of life with someone else at the rudder. This will invariably make the carer feel very ill at ease, and it is important at this point that they stop and assess the situation, talk to the doctor and other friends and family, and see what can be done. Making sure the sufferer sees their doctor regularly to monitor their progress is also very important. If you as a carer feel you have come to a real crisis point, gather as much support as you can from those around you. Try to keep a sense of normality about as much of your life as possible and do not let yourself get isolated.

Probably the hardest emotion to deal with for carers is anger. Some will say you have to keep this hidden in yourself and under control for fear of upsetting the person who is depressed. But this is not alway the best course of action for the sufferer or the carer.

Pent-up anger either comes out in one massive uncontrollable rage which can be very destructive or it is suppressed and turns into stress. This can manifest itself in many ways, but some of the symptoms will include irritability, lack of concentration, nausea, headaches, panic attacks, tiredness, lack of motivation, crying, tightness in the chest, dry mouth and many other things.

Having a short moan every so often, saying you are fed up with the way things are, is far better. Yes, it may upset the depressed person for a while, but you cannot wrap them up in cotton wool all the time. Sometimes it is good to let them know how you feel rather than it always being the other way around.

I mentioned earlier in this chapter about the importance of looking after yourself and giving yourself treats, which we all need, no matter how small. Here is Helen's story, which I hope will make you smile but also understand the importance of having something nice to look forward to.

Helen's husband Chris had become ill due to the pressure that had built up at work. As deputy head teacher at a comprehensive school, he was finding he was doing less and less teching and more administration work, which he hated. The school was in a very rough area and most of the children either came from broken homes or had bad behaviour problems. Being very much left in charge of discipline, Chris found dealing with some of the strong-willed aggressive students too much to cope with. After one of the long summer breaks he found he was unable to return to work; even thinking about it made him shake and feel sick. Over the next few months he became more and more depressed and Helen found his mood swings very hard to cope with. Their own children were scared, and she had to keep him calm and at the same time keep the children's lives on an even keel. Chris always took himself off to bed by nine o'clock and with the children asleep Helen would find herself on her own. This was the time of the day she really looked forward to because each night she would take a large Mars bar, sit on her back doorstep to eat it and look at the sky.

'I know it's daft,' she told me, 'but it is the thought of this that gets me through the day. It's my time. Chris wouldn't understand at the moment, but I am hoping one day soon that he will and we will laugh about this.'

I think this says it all; we all find our own ways of coping with difficult times. Sometimes it is something that might seem insignificant to others, but it works for you and that is what counts.

So far we have looked at carers who are finding their partners' depression hard to cope with. Would you believe that it actually suits some people that their partners are depressed and they collude with them to keep them this way?

Here are four case histories where this is happening, all for different reasons.

Jill is a widow aged 54; her son Philip aged 34 is a vicar. For six years Jill devoted her life to supporting Philip in his ministry. Her happiness depended on his. When Philip said he was taking a six-month sabbatical to go and work in India Jill was devastated, but soon rallied by telling herself and everyone else that she was needed to keep things going while he was away. Two months after his departure he wrote to tell her he had met a really nice girl who was a relief worker.

Jill began to panic! Another woman in his life! When she was contacted a few weeks later to say her son was ill with hepatitis and would be coming home when he was well enough to travel, it seemed almost like a 'divine intervention'. Her son arrived home and she set to looking after him. He was very unwell, and despite his faith he became extremely depressed. His doctor wanted him to go into hospital for a while, mainly to get him away from his mother who he felt was not helping his recovery. She kept telling him he was lucky to have survived but it would be a long haul before he beat the depression – if he ever did, as some people had it for life.

It suited Jill to keep him depressed because it kept him with her, not travelling the world meeting eligible young women who could take him away from her.

Fortunately for Philip his doctor's resolve was stronger than his mother's and he is now on the road to recovery. He still wants to return to India when he is better. As for Jill, she probably needs help more than he does but would never admit it.

Case history 2 is similar but is about Ken and Rachel. Running his own motor business, long hours, little rest and no social life led Ken to be so depressed that he had to stop work and leave things to his brother to run. For years Rachel had been so lonely and the children hardly saw their dad. When Ken became ill she was in no hurry to help him get back to work. For the first time she was in charge, he was at home with her and the children, and the longer she could keep him that way the better she would like it.

Case history 3 is about Valerie who contacted me on one of my radio programmes because she had been suffering with agoraphobia and depression for seven years. This had been brought on through a stressful nursing career when she was overlooked for promotion many times, and she felt the reason was because she was so fat. She had tried dieting but just could not shift the weight; she became depressed, was off sick for months and never returned to her job. She told me she never went out of the house; her husband did everything, including the shopping. She was getting fatter because she ate all the time and did no exercise.

Sometimes she would suggest to her husband that she would like to try to go out but he would always make excuses, saying when she became less depressed he would take her. Then one day she got a phone call from a woman who told her that she had been having an affair with her husband for six years. Now Valerie knew why he never wanted her to go out. If he kept her indoors his secret was safe. Contrary to what she thought Valerie did not get any worse; in fact she was determined to get better. She kept in contact with me for eighteen months. She had told her husband she knew about the other woman and that when she was better she would get a job and leave. We arranged for a psychiatric nurse to visit her regularly to help her with her depression and agoraphobia. She also dieted and lost three stone. The last time she contacted me her husband had left, and she was having counselling and hoped to get a job in a nursing home very soon.

Our last case history for this chapter is a very sad story about Renata and Gerry. When they met Renata was living rough on the streets of London having fled from her parents, who abused her. She had resorted to prostitution to survive and she also had a drug problem. Gerry says when he first saw Renata he fell in love and wanted to take care of her. A year later they were married, they had one daughter and together they started a cleaning business.

Competition from larger companies and the advent of more washable items led to them going bankrupt. Gerry tried to get work but was turned down so many times that he became depressed. Renata looked after him as if he was a baby; she smothered him with so much love and attention that he believed he was going to die and that was why she was being so kind to him. He got worse and worse, until one day he confided in her his fears. Horrified when she realized what he had been thinking, she broke down and said to him, 'You dragged me up from the gutter and I thought this was my chance to pay you back for all you had done for me.'

Being a carer or a friend of someone suffering with depression is never easy. It takes a lot of patience, kindness and strength. Sometimes it is not easy to get it right, but the vast majority do a marvellous job. They are cast into the role of a carer often without warning and definitely with no training, and often with little or no support. Despite this they are the ones who manage to help their loved ones through the dark tunnel of depression and out into the sun again. Their role is vital and it should never be underestimated.

Questions and answers

Q My husband is very depressed and hasn't worked for six weeks. He gets very agitated with the children when they play and raises his voice to them a lot. We live in a small terraced house and it isn't easy to separate the children from him, especially as we only have one sitting room. They are not naughty or particularly noisy but he thinks they should play in their bedrooms all the time while he lounges in front of the TV. To hear him argue with them over which channel should be on makes me realize it is like having an extra child to look after now. What should I do?

A You haven't got a magic wand and so you can't make everything perfect for your husband or the children. Neither should you be expected to. At this point in time it is probably easier to negotiate with your children rather than him. Children are more resilient and adaptable than we give them credit for. If your husband has access to the TV for most of the time then make a rule that between four and six the children get to watch what they want to, and try during this time to encourage him to do something else, perhaps help you with the evening meal, go and have a shower or maybe go out in the garden or for a walk. Then explain to the children that their dad is unwell and needs rest, and that they can help him by playing either in their rooms or out in the garden for some of the time and quietly when in the sitting room. If they could do this then they will be helping both of you. Perhaps let them make suggestions on how they can help as well. Being involved rather than feeling they are being pushed out will bring far better results.

Q I worry every time I go to work because my wife, who has been depressed for over a year, keeps threatening suicide. She won't take her medication and the doctor seems to be unconcerned about the whole thing. She gets aggressive towards me about being made redundant from her job when it has nothing to do with me. I would never forgive myself if anything were to happen to her but I can't give up my job because we need the money.

A Over the years I have come to realize that far more people threaten suicide than actually attempt it, and that if someone is really intent on doing so then they will choose a time when you least expect it so they can carry it through. Of course you are worried, and rightly so, but you can't stop working and sit and watch her all day. It sounds as if communication has broken down between her and her doctor and it might be a good idea to make a fresh start, either with another doctor in the practice or with a new GP altogether. She needs to have confidence in her GP for her to get on the road to recovery. Regular medication might be one area she needs to work on so that she gives the tablets time to work and makes sure she is on the right ones for her.

Q My mother lives alone since my father was killed in an accident. He was suffering with depression after having to take on the work of two colleagues, who had been made redundant, as well as his own. She has become very morbid and depressed. She use to be such a cheerful soul but now she is the opposite. My sister and I have worked out a rota so that Mum has visitors every day; some of these are from Dad's company. We thought Mum would be pleased but it seems to be irritating her, yet she won't say why. My husband says we are being over-sensitive and that her manner is all part of her illness. She had a nice job as a school dinner lady and she will not even think about going back to this. What do you think?

A Your husband could well be right: behaviour patterns do change when a person is depressed and so do their tolerance levels. Although I am sure you mean well, I'm not sure that you should be organizing your mum's help in this way. Maybe she finds it very stressful having this bevy of visitors trailing through her house each week. Being depressed doesn't mean she is totally incapable of knowing what is right for her. Try talking to her and suggest that whether she has visitors or not should be left to her. I think this might help ease the situation.

11

Bring Back the Tea Lady and Get Rid of the Bullies!

When I first went to work, tea breaks were an important and integral part of the working day. Often we would leave the office and spend our 15 minute break at a nearby coffee bar devouring toasted teacakes and discussing the events of the night before. It was a chance to socialize, cement friendships and come back to work feeling refreshed. But even more important in our working day was Elsie, our tea lady, who not only provided her own home-made cakes to go along with tea in the canteen but was also the one we could all turn to when we wanted to share some exciting news or needed a shoulder to cry on. Probably the lowest-paid in the company, she fulfilled one of the most important roles. She knew when to be discreet but was always the fount of information when we wanted to know what was going on in the firm.

When you felt disgruntled and that you were being unfairly treated, ten minutes with Elsie and a cup of her well-brewed tea soon put you to rights. She was a listener and a giver of sound advice, based on her age of 70 years. Managers and underlings like us all found a tea break and a chat with Elsie was a breath of fresh air twice a day. Lunch-times we moaned that she had cooked macaroni cheese for the third time that week, but we ate and enjoyed it as we all had a break from work.

What a difference today! Only a handful of companies have tea ladies, let alone tea breaks! Instead there are machines that noisily dispense cans of soft drinks and hot drinks that look and taste like dishwater. They are also the cause of many people becoming stressed, because employees are not encouraged to take breaks, and drift towards these machines for endless drinks during the day, probably because they see it as a chance to leave their desks, bench or workstation. The result is they drink far too much tea and coffee, and this can affect their stress levels. I once had a lady write to me who was constantly on edge and depressed, and it turned out she was drinking up to 18 cups of coffee a day from the machine at work. When she cut down and eventually drank water instead the symptoms disappeared.

Regular breaks are important, both in reducing susceptibility to depression and for the health of your body as a whole. Sitting, standing or crouching in one position for many hours on end isn't a good idea, and if you can't leave where you work at least stand up and stretch at least once an hour. Don't work and drink at the same time, even if it is only for three or four minutes; stop working, sip your tea, look out of the window, close your eyes . . . anything that helps you relax. I know one lady called Veronica who takes a poem in to work each day and reads it as she drinks her tea. She says if she appeared to stop work her boss would glower at her. This way she switches off for two or three minutes and he doesn't know. If she didn't do this she feels she wouldn't be able to get through the day without becoming anxious and depressed. At lunch-times she goes swimming before having her sandwich which, depending on the weather, she eats while she sits on a bench outside the factory where she works.

Here is the poem for you to share. It's called 'Today' and it was written by a poet called Ella Wheeler Wilcox, who was born in 1850 and died in 1919.

It is said that Ella could do with words what Leonardo da Vinci did with a brush. She had a mastery of expression with words that gave light, hope and creativity upon the dreary, hopeless destructiveness of life. She had a knack of getting to the heart of the most complex of everyday human problems, and then she would come up with the most simply worded yet highly potent answers in verse. I can see why Veronica liked this poem, so here it is.

TODAY

Let me today do something that shall take, a little sadness from
the world's vast store.
And may I be favoured as to make, those I meet feel life holds
more.
However meager be my reward or wealth, let me reach and give
help to all kind
A word of encouragement, a thought to their health, dropped as I
pass for troubled hearts to find . . .
Let me look back across the span, twixt dawn and dusk and
say . . .
Because I have tried to aid my fellow man the World's a better
place today.

Ella Wheeler Wilcox (1850–1919)

Have you noticed how lunch-hours have shrunk over the years and are now referred to as lunch breaks, often lasting as little as half an hour or less? Hardly the chance to gobble down some food before it's time to go back to work. Certainly no time to relax.

Because of the enormous pressures that have built up in the workplace, 'worktalk' seems to have spilled over into the lunch break as well. This is particularly noticeable with the younger employees, who seem to talk non-stop about work during lunch as if their jobs depended on it. This is probably not too far removed from the truth, but it is very worrying because they are putting themselves in a high risk category when it comes to depression and other health problems.

If your employer is against you stopping work to have a tea or coffee break, look at your contract of employment and check that you are not working longer than you should be doing without a break. There are strict guidelines on the number of hours employees are allowed to work before they have a break and the Personnel Department should be able to tell you what these are. If this fails check with the Citizens' Advice Bureau.

Our bodies are pretty capable of coping with most things but they do need rest, even if it's only for a few minutes, so make the most of your lunch break and get some exercise as well as some relaxation. Rushing out to the shops and worrying about what to have for tea is not an ideal way to spend it. Far better to go for a walk, a swim or sit in the fresh air each day.

An important part of the working day is getting on with the people you work with; spending time together in the lunch break, exchanging ideas and views, is a way of relaxing. By doing this you are building up good dynamics between you and your colleagues that will help you to work together and be understanding to each other's difficulties should they arise. Some people are very shy and reserved and find it almost impossible to mix. It is easy for them to be overlooked and left out and this often leads to them being labelled as difficult and oddballs by their collegues, when in fact they are just the opposite. These are often the people who suffer with depression in the workplace when this could be avoided. This is why it is important to create a dynamic with them as well by including them in conversations and inviting them to join you for lunch so that they don't feel excluded.

This is the story of Sam and how his shyness led him to suffer what he calls his invisible illness . . . depression. He has always been a shy, kind-hearted man and, at 48, married with two children, he found he was being ostracized by the other workers because they saw him as being stand-offish whereas in fact he was quiet and shy. You would have thought that as he worked in a hospital people would understand, but the demands made on him by his job and the sneers and comments from the other porters pushed him to the edge and twice he tried to commit suicide. When his colleagues found out about this they talked about him within his hearing, saying he was weak and wicked. He says he feels ashamed of himself and that life at work has become a living nightmare. He is frightened to go to work, and when he is among people there he now has panic attacks and thinks he is being pushed to the edge and is going to die. Yet he continues to suffer in silence, and won't complain about the way others treat him or see his GP because he feels this would mean admitting to himself that he is weak.

A sad story but not an uncommon one, and this is why both employees and employers should recognize when a member of staff is being victimized and has become depressed because of it.

A similar story comes from Jim, who worked in a canning factory. He was taken on to keep an eye on the machinery and rectify any faults. It sounds simple enough, but both his supervisors and the other workers took great exception to this when he grounded machines for safety checks because he believed them to be unsafe. A still machine meant less output and productivity bonus for the supervisors and no overtime for the workers, so they did everything to make his life a misery. They tore up his reports, messed up the machines he had checked and then reported him to the management as incompetent. Things got so bad that he was frightened to go to the toilet, for fear of what they would do when he was away. Even the manager who had employed him began to doubt his capabilities. After all, could all the supervisors and workers be wrong? Was the man a troublemaker? He chose to believe he was, and Jim was called in and given a warning about being uncooperative and causing trouble among his fellow workers. By this time Jim was suffering with depression and had a wife who didn't understand. She just wanted his pay-packet on the table at the end of the week. Eventually Jim was forced to go sick and was off work for eight weeks. During this time he decided he could never return to his job and handed in his notice. Since then he has taken work on an oil-rig; he is no longer depressed and hopes his marriage will last, but being separated while working away is not helping.

Although Jim chose to leave his job and Sam chose to stay, many other depressed people find themselves the victims of unfair or constructive dismissal. If this has happened to you try to do something about it. Speak to a solicitor and see if you have a case for seeking compensation. Although it may be a long and often arduous task try not to let this put you off. Stand up for what you think is right. Because of the reduction in breaks and socializing within the workplace today, it is not so easy to get to know fellow workers or to recognize that some people are the kind to take advantage for their own ends, namely the 'workplace bullies'. We talk about children who are bullies and say how dreadful this is, but adults can be as bad, if not worse. It is a dreadful thing to have to admit, but bullying in the workplace goes on all the time, and what is even worse is that in most cases no one does anything about it. The victim becomes depressed and isolated, and the culprits gain strength from this because in their minds it only goes to prove that their victim is weak and inadequate.

They can't or won't understand that depression is not ageist, sexist or racist and that it is an illness that attacks one in four people at some time in their lives. Bullies in the workplace are inadequate people who protect themselves by projecting their own inadequacies on to other people. By this they avoid facing up to their own shortcomings or doing anything about them. It diverts attention away from themselves on to their victim, and this is how many incompetent workers and managers manage to keep their jobs.

Bullies are two-faced and clever, and when needed they can turn on the charm and lie so convincingly that it's hard for others to believe that they could be cruel to anyone. This is why you have to take steps to protect yourself. Talk to others who are not involved in the bullying about what is going on. Don't bottle it up by trying to cope alone; ask them to watch and decide for themselves what is going on. Complain to your line manager and say you intend to keep a written record of all incidents that occur, so that this way a pattern of the bullying will emerge. Bullies can deny individual incidents but it is harder for them to talk their way out of a pattern of events. In some circumstances it may be a good idea to seek legal advice, and your solicitor may suggest that he sends a letter either to the bully or to your manager requesting an end to the victimization. If you have a union representative get in contact with them and give them a copy of the record of bullying that you have made. Sometimes it is the employer who is the bully; signs of this will include a high turnover of staff and absences due to sickness and stress as well as lots of people taking early retirement. If there is a welfare officer or counsellor available at your place of work, ask to see them. Talking about what is happening will not only help you to clarify the problem in your mind but will also help you feel less alone and more able to deal with the situation.

I firmly believe that there is a greater need now that at any other time for counselling to be available in the workplace.

Every year thousands of working hours and millions of pounds are lost because of employees having to take time off through depression. In most cases this could have been avoided if colleagues had been more understanding or if they had felt there was someone they could talk to who wouldn't try to judge them or try to tell them what to do, which is what many people fear. Counselling is about helping people to recognize their problem areas and to look at their options, and then make their own decisions in their own time. Having counselling available for staff in medium to large companies, even if it was only for one or two days a week, would probably pay for itself very quickly, because I am sure it would reduce the number of people who become depressed.

For smaller companies it would probably not be a viable propostion to have to employ a counsellor on a regular basis, but it doesn't stop them having an arrangement with larger companies to share their counselling services or with a GP practice or private counsellor who they could call upon whenever the need arose. Some large companies such as Marks and Spencer, the Department of Health and British Telecom already have counselling for their staff, and hopefully more will follow their example and see the wisdom of it.

The environment you work in can also affect the way you feel. An untidy, dirty or boring office or place of work can make you feel low and ill at ease. Nicely decorated ones with warmth, good lighting, clean toilets, plants and a seating area for relaxation make going to work more enjoyable and lift a person's spirits.

A psychologist called Hans Eysenck suggests people can be categorized into two personality types, the extroverts, who are sociable, impulsive and like variety in their lives, and the introverts, who are quiet, reserved, plan carefully for the future and may be inclined to be pessimistic and look on the bad side of things. He then suggests that people can be further divided into emotionally stable people who cope better with stress and unstable groups who find it difficult. I tend to think that this is too cut and dried and that circumstances can reduce even the most stable person into a depressed state. It is, however, interesting and helpful to understand yourself, and the following exercise might be helpful.

Look at the list in Figure 13 and pick out six that you feel described you best before you became depressed.

Figure 13

- Sociable
- Talkative
- Easygoing
- Careful
- Reliable
- Calm
- Moody
- Anxious

- Quiet
- Touchy
- Even-tempered
- Thoughtful
- Optimistic
- Active
- Reserved
- Excitable

- Aggressive
- Leadership
- Impulsive
- Restless
- Rigid
- Responsive
- Unreliable
- Unsociable

Once you have done this do the same thing again, but this time as you feel it describes you now that you are depressed. Don't worry if there is a vast difference in the two. That's only to be expected when you are feeling unwell, but it will give you a better understanding of where you are at the present time.

After he became depressed through pressure at work I got Paul to do this exercise (see Figure 14). He described himself before he became depressed as

- sociable;
- optimistic;

- talkative;
- reliable;
- careful;
- leadership.

During his depression this changed to

- unsociable;
- quiet;
- anxious;
- unreliable;
- touchy;
- restless.

After he recovered and went back to work, he reverted to a couple of his original qualities, reliable and careful, but felt talkative, leadership, sociable and optimistic were things of the past. This time he described himself as calm, easygoing, even-tempered and thoughtful.

Figure 14

Original list

Careful	✓
Reliable	✓
~~Optimistic~~	Calm
~~Sociable~~	Easygoing
~~Talkative~~	Even-tempered
~~Leadership~~	Thoughtful

Looking at this latest list after getting over his depression Paul felt it showed that he had struck a happy medium now between the extrovert he used to be and the introvert he became while depressed. He was happy with this and got himself a job within the same company, but had less pressure. He jokingly told me that he missed having a key to the executive toilet but could do without all the stresses and strains his previous post had given him.

Stephie's experience, on the other hand, was entirely different. She described herself before her depression as

- moody;
- anxious;
- quiet;
- touchy;
- restless;
- unreliable.

The only change when she became depressed was that she refused to alter her original list but insisted on adding two more. One – aggressive – from the main list and one of her own choice – swearing – which she said she was becoming a dab hand at.

Three months later she was definitely less depressed. She completely abandoned our original exercise and brought with her her own list which included 'now proficient at swearing', 'have told my mother to stop organizing my life', 'decided to be celibate for a year', 'bought some condoms in case I change my mind', 'have stopped feeling guilty for being me', 'intend to retrain for a different job', 'have stopped sticking pins in an effigy of my old boss . . . he isn't worth the effort'.

I think we can safely say that Stephanie is well on the way to getting better!

Questions and answers

Q I am a 38-year-old married man with three children. My problems started two years ago and became so severe that I suffered in silence in a reclusive manner. Life seems to hold nothing for me any longer. I feel depressed and my physical symptoms, which are many, include sweating, headaches, poor appetite, insomnia and a deep sense of sadness. Ironically I am employed in a caring profession but feel the pressures of working here are so great. I feel social phobia and depression should be taken very seriously because it is a dangerous illness. I am presently off work with depression and social phobia and may never return to work again. I just don't know where my life is going.

A Never . . . is a long time, so don't look beyond the present for a while. See your doctor if you haven't already done so and concentrate on relaxing and giving yourself some tender loving care. Relaxation tapes, meditation and yoga will all help if you feel inclined to give these a try, and so will allowing yourself time to recover without feeling guilty about this. At 38 you have a whole life ahead of you and, believe me, the time will come when you will be able to return to work. Maybe not to the same job but one that you will enjoy.

Q I was off work with depression for several months, and on my return I found someone else doing my job and was sent to another department. I accepted this as I was only too pleased to have recovered and to be managing to work again. The work was similar and I thought I was coping well. People were not all that friendly but I put that down to them not knowing me very well. A month after I returned my new manager said there was a staff meeting and I had to attend. I was shocked when the manager said I was behind with my work and that others had to help me out. That caused an uproar because they all said they had enough to do. To my horror he then explained I had been off work with depression and that everyone had to make allowances for me. I sat there not knowing where to put myself, I felt so humiliated. I have to say everyone has been kind and helpful to me since and my manager says I am doing well. But I feel like a charity case that they are having to put up with.

A Your boss may not have been at the front of the queue when tact was given out but at least his heart is in the right place. He could have managed this in a more discreet way but at least you don't have any secrets hidden away and people are being understanding, which is what you need. There is an old saying that 'what's news today is forgotten tomorrow'. Stop worrying and everything will be fine.

12

Hope for the Future

Dear Friend,

'The world is a lovely place and well worth fighting for.' That is the opinion of Andy. Despite being made redundant five times through no fault of his own he had managed to find an inner strength to cope with his depression, and so can you.

We have travelled a long way together through the pages of this book and I hope that it hasn't been too painful an experience for you. Your depression is probably one of the worst periods of your life, and in many ways it is worse than a physical illness because it affects the whole mind and body.

Once it has you in its clutches it feels as if it will never let you go but, believe me, that isn't true. There is a light at the end of the tunnel and step by step, however slowly, you will find it. There may be many setbacks and adjustments to make, but keep your mind firmly fixed on recovering and you will. All illnesses run their span and depression is no different. With the medication, counselling and therapies available to us today no one should feel there is no hope for them, but it may mean asking for help so don't be ashamed to do this.

People often say that depressed people are self-pitiers and, yes, it is possible to reach a stage when you do feel like this, but never listen to anyone who says that you are weak, inadequate or that you have brought this upon yourself, because that is rubbish.

We know that depression is caused by a chemical imbalance in the brain and that individual circumstances can trigger this off, but that isn't a weakness – it is just another medical condition that seems to have gathered shame and stigma over the years through people's lack of information and fear of anything to do with mental illness.

It is as if they are scared that in some way it reflects on them or it could be catching. People shun things they don't understand because of fear. Today we read more in the press and hear and see programmes about depression on radio and television. It's coming out of the 'closet', and this will help people to accept and understand that it can happen to anyone without warning, including themselves, and that it is an illness and nothing to be ashamed of.

We still have a long way to go in the workplace for employers to fully understand and support staff who have become depressed, whether it has been caused by the job or not. But things are moving for the better and hopefully will continue to do so. It is a constantly changing situation, but the sooner all employers realize that the more stress they put on their staff the more likely they are to become ill and depressed, the better.

Frederick Herzberg, a US clinical psychologist, was born in 1923 and became Professor of Management at Utah University. Having been posted to Dachau concentration camp after it had been liberated he believed that mental health is the core issue of our times. On his return to the United States he worked in the US Public Health Service. His work focused on the individual in the workplace but it became popular with managers as well because it emphasized the importance of managers' knowledge and expertise. In 1959 he published a book called *Motivation to Work* (Chapman, 1959) in which he wrote about his hygiene and motivation theory. This suggested that the work situation can be divided into two areas for concern. The first he called the 'hygiene or maintenance factors' with these being the areas that cause dissatisfaction in work, such as pay and working conditions. The second are the elements of work which motivate people, such as recognition, responsibility, achievement and promotion. These are called 'motivators' and Herzberg believed that if these factors were taken on board by management and used as a minimum standard required for employees, motivation would be greatly improved and workers would be much happier.

For example, if this theory is to be followed, under the 'maintenance and hygiene' area there should be the provision of a nice working environment with good heating and lighting and wherever possible good leisure or recreational facilities. Adequate parking should be provided and good canteen facilities or arrangements for sandwiches or other foods to be delivered to the workplace, especially those that are in more isolated places.

Under the 'motivators' area employers should ensure that their staff feel valued, that payment for the work they are doing is fair and that good pension and health facilities are in place. This will go a long way to giving workers self-esteem and reduce the number of people who get depressed in the workplace.

It is a pity more employers don't follow his ideas. Perhaps it is time to make a poster and put it above where you work saying 'Happy workers produce more work'. No one can honestly dispute this, and it might just make a few employers think.

Two of my readers, Tim and Karen, went through agonizing periods of stress and depression caused by their work but came through it.

I was really pleased when Tim wrote to say, 'Having suffered badly with depression and being unable to return to work I am now really succeeding.'

He is studying for a degree in behavioural science, getting really good grades, and is researching suicide for his dissertation in the hope of doing post-graduate research into depression and suicide. What an achievement after such a bad period of his life.

As for Karen, who had many problems, she wrote to say, 'I have gone back to a different job now. I am a different person, a better person, a more caring person. Just as cancer sufferers often say that they are glad they have had the disease because it made them take stock of their lives, the same thing has happened to me. A new me has emerged and I am now looking ahead with new career aspirations, better relationships and above all I try to get rid of negatives and concentrate on the positive side of life. I am happy to say that I have recovered mentally and physically from the trauma with the help of family, friends and a psychologist.'

The road to recovery from depression is a stony one to tread but it teaches lessons with every step. You won't be the same person when you reach the end of it but you could well be a better one. Not for you the critical view of others who can't cope – depression will have given you a greater understanding of other people's fears and feelings. You will also recognize your strengths and weaknesses and know that whatever comes your way you will do your best to cope. You will get better, so don't feel ashamed or alone. It isn't your fault and we all love you.

Learning to accept yourself and your depression is an important part of the journey, and one way of doing this is to try and see it from another person's point of view. Try to think what you would say to someone you care about who felt depressed. Words of encouragement would probably spring to your lips. Well, try doing this to yourself. Every time you feel low, tell yourself that this will pass, it's just another stone on the path that you can overcome. And find a lot of love for yourself as well. Depressed people are far too hard on themselves; they feel unloved and compound this by disliking or even hating themselves. You are loveable, and if you can begin to love yourself again the door will close on your depression.

You won't take life for granted any more, and as you come out of the tunnel of dark depression the sun will be shining at the other end.

Let me leave you with part of a poem that was written by an American poet, David Bates, in 1850.

Speak Gently

Speak gently, to those who feel poorly.
Know they may have toiled in vain.
Perchance unkindness made them so,
Oh! win them back again!

Speak gently, kindly to those whose minds feel poorly.
Let no harsh unfair tone be heard.
They have enough that they must endure,
Without unkind thoughts and words.

I think it sums up very nicely how we should treat those who become depressed through no fault of their own.
Take care.
Kindest regards,

Vicky